BE COMFORTED

Be Comforted

HEALING IN TIMES OF
LOSS
ANGER
ANXIETY
LONELINESS
SICKNESS
DEATH

GLORIA HUTCHINSON

ST. ANTHONY MESSENGER PRESS
Cincinnati, Ohio

Scripture citations are taken from the *New Revised Standard Version Bible*, copyright ©1989 by the Division of Christian Education of the National Council of the Churches of Christ in the U.S.A., and used by permission. All rights reserved.

Cover and book design by Mark Sullivan

Library of Congress Cataloging-in-Publication Data

Hutchinson, Gloria.
    Be comforted : healing in times of loss, anger, anxiety, loneliness, sickness,
  death / by Gloria Hutchinson.
        p. cm.
    Includes bibliographical references.
    ISBN 0-86716-550-2 (alk. paper)
    1. Consolation.   I. Title.
  BV4905.3.H87 2004
  242'.4—dc22

2004015902

ISBN 0-86716-550-2

Published by St. Anthony Messenger Press
www.AmericanCatholic.org
Printed in the U.S.A.

for David and Lisa,
kind comforters

"EVERY PROVERB, EVERY BOOK, EVERY BY-WORD THAT BELONGS TO THEE FOR AID OR COMFORT, SHALL SURELY COME HOME THROUGH OPEN OR WINDING PASSAGES."

—Ralph Waldo Emerson

CONTENTS

Introduction

"COMFORT, O COMFORT MY PEOPLE,
SAYS YOUR GOD."
—Isaiah 40:1

Whenever I hear Jesus advising his friends not to worry about tomorrow because today's trouble will more than suffice for now, I comment ruefully, "You said a mouthful there, rabbi." At least we cannot claim that he promised us a highway to heaven with no breakdown lane. As he suffered, so do we. But there are times when we suspect that we are doing a lot more sowing in tears than reaping in rejoicing. That's the point at which being comforted becomes a necessity if we and our faith are to remain intact.

Although some of the superzealous saints sought out suffering for its own sake, most of us have no need to go looking for it. Let Simon Stylites perch on his pillar, Peter Damian flog his own back, and Francis of Assisi roll naked in the snow. We trust that there is plenty of disciplinary trouble to go around right in our homes and workplaces, our parishes and communities, our terror-shrouded world. In our response to the suffering that seeks us out, we, by God's grace, forge our unique sanctity.

The merciless pace, pervasive materialism, and technological impersonalism of American society take their daily toll in divorces, cancer, depression and alienation. Many recognize where the Jesuit poet Gerard Manley Hopkins was coming from when he wrote: "Comforter, where, where is your comforting?"[1] However, we also know, as Hopkins did, that believing prayer will not forever seem to be "like dead letters sent / to dearest him that lives alas! away."[2] The Christ who prayed Lazarus out of the tomb cannot be helpless against whatever ails our bodies, minds or spirits. He will not fail us.

We can, however, fail him by nursing the delusion that suffering is an unjust intrusion on our happiness, a glitch in the master plan. One way to convince ourselves of this truth is to make a ruthlessly honest self-examination in which we ask: How have my experiences of suffering changed me? How have pain and loss contributed to my spiritual maturity? Am I wiser, more compassionate, stronger and more firmly rooted in my faith?

We readily romanticize the image of God as the Potter ("Just like the clay in the potter's hand, so are you in my hand, O house of Israel" or in the version popularized by Carey Landry in his song "Abba! Father!" "You are the potter; we are the clay," both from Jeremiah 18:6).

But we forget that this appealing image is preceded by the Lord's sending his prophet down to the potter's house. There Jeremiah observes the craftsman at work: "The vessel he was making of clay was spoiled in the potter's hand, and he reworked it into another vessel, as seemed good to him" (18:4). This reworking of the clay to better suit the Potter's purpose must be done with firm hands.

Often enough when various sorrows have come knocking at my door, I have called out, "Go away! There's nobody home." I would prefer that they come back at a more convenient time or pass me by all together. Meister Eckhart, however, does not allow me to get away with such a short-

. . . . .

"WHAT CANNOT BE ALTERED MUST BE BORNE, NOT BLAMED."
—Thomas Fuller, M.D.

. . . . .

"BLISS IS LASTING; PAIN IS PASSING."
—Julian of Norwich

. . . . .

sighted approach. "If you think you can be God's Son [or daughter] and not suffer, you are mistaken. It is written in the Book of Wisdom that God tries and proves the just [person] as gold is tried in the burning of the furnace."[3]

The degree of our suffering is dependent on how we embrace or deny it, wade through or attempt to circumvent it. The choice is ours. Yet, until we are tested by multiple sorrows arriving like loathsome guests for unlimited stays, we may not realize how crucial it is to be prepared for their appearance.

Be Comforted is a guidebook for those who are trudging through the swamp of unelected sorrows right now. It is also intended for those who, like the wise virgins, want to be sure that they have plenty of oil for their lamps come midnight.

This book was conceived a few years ago when the editorial director of St. Anthony Messenger Press returned from an international book fair. She was troubled by several strangers she met there who, over the course of a week, shared their heartaches with her. Lisa Biedenbach commented, "It was upsetting because they needed more comfort than I could give." That was the seed the Spirit watered as I reflected on my own sources of consolation in assorted trials.

Although the following chapters separate our sufferings into categories, in reality, they often attack us two or more at a time. Thus, an unsuspecting host may have to confront a divorce with its attendant anger and inevitable loneliness all at the same time.

Likewise, the six sources of comfort marked off in each chapter spill over into each other's domain. They are divided for the sake of ready reference into: Story Time, Scriptural Voices, Spiritual Kin, Creative Works, Contemporary Spirituality, and Holy Laughter. The opening narrative is a nod to the child in us who, in times of distress or vulnerability, can be comforted by "Once upon a

. . . . .

"THE GREATER PART OF OUR HAPPINESS OR MISERY DEPENDS ON OUR DISPOSITIONS, AND NOT ON OUR CIRCUMSTANCES."
—Martha Washington

. . . . .

"BE JOYFUL THOUGH YOU HAVE CONSIDERED ALL THE FACTS."
—Wendell Berry

. . . . .

time…" Life urges us to draw on every source of relief rather than saying "No thank you" to those we had not thought of trying.

In his stories of the Hasidic masters, Elie Wiesel tells us of Rabbi David Leikes who was known for his contagious joy. It was not that the rabbi was a stranger to suffering. He lived long enough to mourn his wife and seven children. Yet sorrow never defeated him. "To praise God, one must live, he said, and to live, one must enjoy life in spite of life."[4]

When my eyes rested on the rabbi's words in a time of multiple troubles, I recognized them as a personal blessing. *Be Comforted* is an attempt to pass it on.

NOTES

1. "No worst, there is none," Gerard Manley Hopkins, quoted in Peter Milward, S.J., *A Commentary on the Sonnets of G. M. Hopkins* (Chicago: Loyola University Press, 1969), p. 146.

2. "I wake and feel," *Ibid.*, p. 158.

3. Raymond Bernard Blakney, *Meister Eckhart: A Modern Translation* (New York: Harper & Row, 1941), p. 65.

4. Elie Wiesel, *Souls on Fire: Portraits and Legends of Hasidic Masters* (New York: Simon & Schuster, 1972), p. 45.

One

Be Comforted in Your Loss
A healing chapter for the divorced

"THE ONE WHO TRUSTS THE LORD WILL NOT SUFFER LOSS."
—SIRACH 32:24

. . . . .

STORY TIME

She is on her way from a retreat in a distant parish to a friend's new home. On her lap are the e-mailed directions from Emily, guiding her from Bangor to Gorham. Her breathing is shallow. She is anxious as a blind person venturing out for the first time with a seeing-eye dog. As the Portland traffic picks up, her grip on the steering wheel tightens.

Ever since her husband of thirty years filed for a divorce, driving has become hazardous duty for her. She often stops to ask for directions, and promptly forgets them. A four-hour trip takes six because she repeatedly misses her exit on the turnpike. Even if she sees the exit sign, she cannot trust that it is the right one.

Now she finds herself at a traffic light where Emily's directions leave her marooned. Left? Right? Her indecision prompts strident urban honking behind her. Hands shaking, she pulls into a Dunkin' Donuts parking lot and calls her friend.

At the sound of Emily's voice, the driver sobs like a toddler lost in a department store. "I don't know where I am. Somewhere in Portland," she says, looking around for a street sign. The maternal reassurances and repeated directions from Emily are offered in a language she can no longer understand. "Either you'll have to come get me or I'm going home," she insists, as though she could find her way home. "You stay right there," says Emily. "I'll be there in ten minutes." The driver slumps over the steering wheel, drowning in her own inadequacy.

Emily, ever confident in the domestic fortress of her husband and eight children, soon arrives to rescue her. However, before leaving the parking lot, she rushes out to embrace her friend, make her laugh, assure her that coming to get her "is no trouble at all."

Only later does the divorced woman learn from others who have "been there" that being physically lost is a common tribulation in the first stages of spousal loss. Whether the husband was a skilled navigator or not, his empty seat in the car symbolizes abandonment. The discarded wife cannot get her bearings. Having lost her accustomed way in life, she is thrashing through the woods without a compass.

She had not expected that divorce would feel so much like death. Every common chore from driving to grocery shopping now loomed like a high-jump crossbar set at Olympic heights. Insomnia had her groaning with the psalmist, "I lie awake; I am like a lonely bird on the housetop" (Psalm 102:7). Her prayer was angry, accompanied by pounding on the wall: "Where are you when I need you the most? I don't see you wiping every tear from my eye!"

The One she addressed answered her in ways she did not expect and at times not of her own dictation.

SCRIPTURAL VOICES

Jesus never endured the heartbreak of divorce. But he willingly accepted the loss of a potential wife and children in order to give himself completely as an urgent witness to the reign of God. He accepted in advance the loss of a helpmate, a Mary, a Martha, or a Magdalene to share his sleeping mat, to hold him in the night when he cried out against the enemies who were hemming him in.

He says to all of us who have lost a husband or wife, "If any want to become my followers, let them deny themselves and take up their cross daily and follow me. For those who want to save their life will lose it, and those who lose their life for my sake will save it" (Luke 9:23–24).

To those who have lost the homes we lived in and made our own for many years, Jesus says quietly, "Foxes have holes, and birds of the air have nests, but the Son of Man has nowhere to lay his head" (Matthew 8:20). We can choose to hear this as a reminder that whether we wind up

· · · · ·

"ONE KNOWS WHAT ONE HAS LOST, BUT NOT WHAT ONE MAY FIND."
—George Sand

· · · · ·

"MANY WOULD BE WILLING TO HAVE AFFLICTIONS PROVIDED THAT THEY BE NOT INCONVENIENCED BY THEM."
—Francis de Sales

· · · · ·

in a condo or a mobile home, we will still have more than he claimed for himself. When it comes down to it, he is the home that no one can take from us.

Jesus' words of comfort are sharp-edged. They are the "pebble in our shoe." If we accept them, we have no choice but to see beyond the present loss, believe in what lies ahead. He reaches out a hand to us and says, "Take heart, it is I" (Matthew 14:27). Although we are convinced that we do not know how, we step out of the boat, in which we had placed our entire security, and tread gingerly on the water, trying not to look down, trying not to be cowed by the wind on the open sea.

We have lost the life we thought we would always have. Unless we let it go, our arms cannot embrace whatever life God has in store for us. Only by relaxing our grip on the steering wheel can we find our way.

Adapting what E.L. Doctorow had to say about writing a novel, we can remember that "Getting through a [divorce] is like driving a car at night. You can see only as far as your headlights, but you can make the whole trip that way."

Spiritual Kin

Whether or not we have spiritual kin among our own families and friends, there is always an entire communion of saints waiting to be summoned to our aid. Some of them are separation or divorce survivors, like Rose Hawthorne Lathrop (1851–1926), foundress of the Servants of Relief for Incurable Cancer, and Baroness Catherine de Hueck Doherty (1896–1985), foundress of Madonna House and author of *Poustinia*. Their witness is one of God's manifold ways of being here to comfort us.

Consider inviting Dorothy Day (1897–1980) over for a cup of coffee. Ask her about her young adult years before she co-founded the Catholic Worker with Peter Maurin. Find out how she survived not only a legal divorce from her first short-term husband, but how she lived with the chronic

. . . . .

"There is nothing in this world which may be clung to blamelessly."
—Rama IV

. . . . .

"We are all in the same boat in a stormy sea and we owe each other a terrible loyalty."
—G.K. Chesterton

. . . . .

pain of separation from Forster Batterham, her common-law husband and father of their child, Tamar.

Listen as Dorothy tells you about the days and nights of yearning for Forster, whom she had deeply loved. When both Dorothy and Tamar were baptized into the Catholic Church, Forster, an atheist, could no longer be a part of their lives. Faced with a choice between God and man, Dorothy chose God. She later wrote:

> I had known enough of love to know that a good healthy family life was as near to heaven as one could get in this life. There was another sample of heaven, of the enjoyment of God. The very sexual act itself was used again and again in Scripture as a figure of the beatific vision. It was not because I was tired of sex, satiated, disillusioned, that I turned to God. Radical friends used to insinuate this. It was because through a whole love, both physical and spiritual, I came to know God.[1]

. . . . .

"FLEE TO GOD AND WE SHALL BE COMFORTED."
—Julian of Norwich

. . . . .

Dorothy Day learned how to live without the husband who had been her daily companion. She let Forster go, wrapping her life around Jesus and his least ones. She prayed, received Communion daily, made retreats, read great books, lived with those who came in off the streets, served the soup, led peace vigils, joined anti-war demonstrations, went to prison and lived to enjoy her great-grandchildren.

During the many years of her long loneliness, Dorothy became a powerful witness to her belief that every person is to be welcomed into our lives as Christ. Especially when those we welcome are strangers or unlike us, we can admit them "Not because it might be Christ who stays with us…Not because these people remind us of Christ…but because they *are* Christ."[2]

In comforting the homeless, the hungry, the mentally adrift, Dorothy Day received God's daily consolation. She was raised from the death of a torturous divorce.

CREATIVE WORKS

In the summer of 2003, book reviews of *The New Work of Dogs: Tending to Life, Love, and Family* by Jon Katz appeared everywhere. The author had studied the increasing dependence of dog owners on their pets to satisfy emotional needs. Katz discovered in his interviews that many owners were relying on their pets to take up the emotional slack left by failed relationships or other losses. He pointed out that increasing divorce rates were among the societal factors raising our reliance on a dog's faithful companionship.

Katz's book led me to share the following story which is partially factual, and completely true.

One night when he came home from work, his daughter was waiting for him. She was holding what appeared to be a baby fox. "What do you think?" Annie asked.

"That depends," he said. "What is it?"

"It's a Pomeranian," she laughed, handing him the long-haired, fox-colored, weasel-faced puppy. He held him out at arm's length and felt him shaking with excitement or fear. Annie assured him that the puppy was already housebroken. "You can drop him off on your way to work and he can spend the day with me and the kids," she assured him. "Then you can pick him up on the way home."

He had never owned a dog. But if he had, he was sure it would have been of a manlier breed. An Irish wolfhound, perhaps, or a black lab. Certainly not the kind of dog associated with rich widows or retired librarians. He wanted to say how impractical and inappropriate the whole thing was. But as he held the creature closer to calm him, he felt a tiny heart beating wildly. "Don't worry, fella," he heard himself saying. "I'll take good care of you."

. . . . .

"RECOLLECT THAT THE ALMIGHTY, WHO GAVE THE DOG TO BE COMPANION OF OUR PLEASURES... HATH INVESTED HIM WITH A NATURE NOBLE AND INCAPABLE OF DECEIT."
—Sir Walter Scott

. . . . .

Grinning at the dog's pointed features and feral black eyes, he observed, "Actually you look more like a weasel than a fox. So that's what I'll call you. None of those fluffy or effeminate names for you, buddy."

Having named the creature, the man was owned. Feeding, walking, brushing and transporting Weasel became daily chores. At least the man called these activities chores. He knew they were much more.

A few weeks later, on a Sunday morning, the man found himself standing in the kitchen, staring at the tiled floor. He ached for his wife, for the familiar routine of blueberry pancakes after church, for the shared reading of the *New York Times* that could take all day if nothing else demanded their attention. A sob startled him. He straightened up, took control of himself.

Weasel bobbed his front paws in a begging gesture. "What do you want, boy? I know you're not hungry and you've already been out," said the man, picking up his mute companion. He sunk his lonely fingers deep into the Pomeranian's pleasurable coat and stroked his tufted ears. The dog laid his head on the man's shoulder. He left it right there while the man wept.

Whatever the source of our loss, a dog or a cat (if it is not terminally independent) can be God's gift of daily consolation. Just as trained therapy dogs draw the sick and elderly out of isolation, warm-bodied Weasels can keep us in practice at loving, providing for, tending and delighting in another.

As *The New Work of Dogs* reveals, the only serious problem presented by our emotional investment in our canine friends arises when we forget that they are loving us in return. We cannot be like the widow who lavished love on her dog after her husband's death. When she remarried, her loyalty to her "best friend" foundered. The dog was no longer taken for daily walks or provided with attentive care. Good stewardship of God's creation requires us to continue loving and pro-

. . . . .

"ALL SPIRITUAL INTERESTS ARE SUPPORTED BY ANIMAL LIFE."
—George Santayana

. . . . .

viding for the pets who have remained at our sides throughout the dark days when our need for them was greatest.

For an appreciation of mutually loving relationships between people and the animals who live with them, I look to *Celtic Prayers* collected by Robert Van der Weyer. In my own loss, I gain solace by reading aloud "The Hermit and His Blackbird" or "The Scholar and His Cat." I am reminded by "The Hunter and the Hunted" that I should "treat God's creatures / As I want others to treat me."[3] I am reminded not to give the dear dog who comforts me any less love should someone come along who gives me more.

Contemporary Wisdom

In the comic film *Parenthood*, one of the characters is a middle-aged mother of two who is divorced. She is a loving, if sometimes addled, parent who remains close to her extended family. During one family gathering, a humorous incident reveals to her brother how much she misses the sexual intimacy of her married life.

Many divorced Catholics who have not remarried will instantly empathize with this character's predicament. The absence of a sexual partner can be a deep suffering—especially for those whose church has yet to widely teach a positive and life-giving spirituality of sexual maturity.

However, there is solid comfort to be found in Ronald Rolheiser's *The Holy Longing: The Search for a Christian Spirituality*. Rolheiser, an Oblate of Mary Immaculate, is a priest-theologian and a specialist in spirituality. He is a gifted integrator of Church teaching with an authentic awareness of contemporary life as most of us experience it.

Consider inviting Ronald Rolheiser, through his book or his lectures, to share with you his reassuringly human understanding of how sexuality "is the engine that drives everything else, body and spirit."[4] Hear his conviction that "Having sex is admittedly not the whole reality of sex, but it is perhaps God's greatest gift to the planet and it offers

. . . . .

"God wishes that we should succor [all creatures] whenever they require it."
—Francis of Assisi

. . . . .

"God is voluptuous and delicious."
—Meister Eckhart

. . . . .

humans the opportunity for genuine intimacy available this side of eternity."[5]

Rolheiser presents a detailed Christian definition of sexuality, with its multiple dimensions of parenting, doing creative work, savoring life, offering service, sharing table companionship, connecting with others in ways that lessen the pain of our separateness.

This expanded awareness of the scope of sexuality leads Rolheiser to an intriguing interpretation of Jesus' response to the oft-married woman who wondered which of her many husbands she would belong to after the resurrection. Jesus informed her "those who are deemed worthy to attain to the coming age and to the resurrection neither marry nor are given in marriage" (Luke 20:35).

Does this remark mean that obligatory celibacy will be practiced in heaven, or that resurrected bodies have no need for sexual expression?

Rolheiser proclaims the good news that "in heaven, all will be married to all."[6] He explains that our surprisingly wide and deep sexual hungers will all be met because our desire to be one with "the universe and everything in it" will finally be satisfied. There will be no more separateness, loneliness, disunity. We will realize ourselves as members of the one Body of Christ.

Therefore, we can take comfort in a spirituality that neither denies nor buries our sexual nature. We can pray for the courage to be one with our God in consistent times of solitude. And we can learn that, as John Powell put it, "happiness is an inside job."

Even if the ideal partner does appear on our now-vacant horizon, he or she cannot bear the burden of our happiness. "Happy are those who love you," Tobit says to the Lord (13:14), and "Blessed are the merciful, for they will receive mercy" says the Lord to us (Matthew 5:7).

Our happiness, whether we are divorced, married, single or celibate, comes from loving God and others. "We

> . . . . .
>
> "THE SOUL IS KISSED BY GOD IN ITS INNERMOST REGIONS."
> —Hildegard of Bingen
>
> . . . . .
>
> "[HUMANITY] HAS IMAGINED A HEAVEN, AND HAS LEFT ENTIRELY OUT OF IT THE SUPREMEST OF ALL HIS DELIGHTS . . . SEXUAL INTERCOURSE!"
> —Mark Twain
>
> . . . . .

love because he first loved us" (1 John 4:19). And in loving as he does, we are made whole, healed, happy.

Holy Laughter/Leisure

When we are learning to live with the reality of a divorce, leisure might seem to be the last thing in which to seek comfort. Most of us bury ourselves neck-deep in work, turning our jobs into Linus's blanket. We ache less when absorbed in the secure routines and demands of what we call "making a living."

Should we begin to suspect that our workaholism might not qualify as a virtue, tradition appears to assure us. Who does not know the Benedictine motto, "To pray is to work, to work is to pray"? Saint Camillus de Lellis had no qualms about claiming that "The true apostolic life consists in giving oneself no rest or repose." Neither Benedict nor Camillus, however, would advise that habitual overwork as a hedge against reality is prayerful or virtuous. Work's primary purpose is to give glory to God by cooperating with him in creation. It is not to hide from the psychic pain of that which must be felt before it can be healed.

Particularly in times of loss, our maternal Creator wants to comfort us in labor's counterpart of holy leisure. The psalmist gives us a simple image:

> But I have calmed and quieted my soul,
>   like a weaned child with its mother;
>   my soul is like the weaned child that is
>   with me.
> (Psalm 131:2)

When we picture ourselves as that contented child on its mother's lap, we get a glimpse of the Sabbath rest God intends us to enjoy—not just on the seventh day, but whenever we need divine comforting. Catholic philosopher Josef Pieper reminds us that leisure and contemplation are playmates, and that the divine wisdom, Sophia herself, continues to play before the Lord.

· · · · ·

"We are healed of a suffering only by experiencing it to the full."
—Marcel Proust

· · · · ·

Pieper defines leisure as "an attitude of mind, a condition of the soul" which is not an automatic result of taking time off from work.[7] The person at true leisure is the opposite of the person at work as toil or economic necessity. It is, he says, "an attitude of non-activity, of inward calm, of silence; it means not being 'busy,' but letting things happen."[8] Leisure embraces celebration, worship, and creation. It is healthful for the soul, the mind, and the body.

Because the divorced person often feels broken, rejected, even worthless, he or she needs to feel God's recreative love in as many ways as possible. We are healed by soaking in the warm conviction of our own loveableness. However, for most of us, it takes courage to sit still in God's presence.

One of my favorite Thomas Merton stories, told by James Finley, relates how Finley, as a young Trappist novice, was straining mightily to practice contemplative prayer. He sought guidance from Merton who was then the novice master. Merton inquired, "How does an apple ripen?" Finley waited, knowing that Merton would answer his own question. "It just sits in the sun."[9]

Like the weaned child on its mother's lap, the apple sitting in the sun is an apt image of holy leisure. When we have not tried it, we might assume that there's nothing to it. However, if we habitually sidetrack our sorrows in TV sitcoms, endless E-mail, or Harlequin romances, twenty minutes of silent sitting, stripped of distractions, requires a brave and generous heart.

Not only do we not want our pain to rise to the surface. We may be laying up guilt about the causes of our divorce. If so, whether the guilt is genuine or not, we avoid "bringing it to God's attention"—or our own. Refusing to recognize either the pain or the guilt is depriving ourselves of the Healer's cleansing light. It is a failure to practice healthful self-love.

. . . . .

"LEISURE IS ABOUT RECOVERING OUR FREEDOM."
—Monika Ghosh

. . . . .

"THE BEST PRAYER IS TO REST IN THE GOODNESS OF GOD KNOWING THAT THAT GOODNESS CAN REACH RIGHT DOWN TO OUR LOWEST DEPTHS OF NEED."
—Julian of Norwich

. . . . .

If sitting contentedly in God's gaze is beyond us, we can work our way up to it with warm-up exercises in holy leisure. These practices can be as varied as our DNA. But here are a few suggestions from reliable sources:

Go fishing when you have no need to catch anything. Sit on a riverbank or wade in a stream. Choose a quiet companion or be a solitary fisherman or woman. As a girl, Therese of Lisieux shared this practice with her father. She never caught anything but simply enjoyed nature's tranquility and the Creator's palpable presence.

Meditate on a poem that expresses your experience of loss and sorrow, or of guarded hope for the new life that awaits you. Consider: "One Art" by Elizabeth Bishop, "The Road Not Taken" by Robert Frost, "A Summer Day" by Mary Oliver, "I Loved You" by Alexander Pushkin, or "Suffering" by Jessica Powers. Let the poem become your prayer for healing. When you are ready, write your own poem in a journal.

Become a vigilant watcher of sunrises and sunsets, thundershowers and snowstorms, stars and cloud formations. Allow yourself to be entranced by the fertile beauty of God in his creation. Gerard Manley Hopkins often subjected his depressed moods and feelings of deprivation to Nature's salutary touch. Medicated with spring breezes, the sight of frolicking lambs, the touch of pear tree leaves, he exclaims: "What is all this juice and all this joy?"[10] (Isn't that what we are missing in our newly unwed state?)

Like learning a foreign language, becoming proficient in holy leisure can be frustrating at first. However, the investment pays off in the joy of acquiring a valuable new skill. We begin to experience the love God lavishes on us at every moment, the love that ripens us at our leisure.

. . . . .

"I HAVE LAID ASIDE BUSINESS, AND GONE A-FISHING."
—Izaak Walton

. . . . .

"ALL PRAISE BE YOURS, MY LORD, THROUGH BROTHERS WIND AND AIR, AND FAIR AND STORMY... MOODS"
—Francis of Assisi

. . . . .

REFLECT

How will you complete this statement: The loss of a husband or wife through divorce is like...?

How will you trust the Lord and cooperate with him in seeking the comfort you need?

PRAY
O Divine Comforter,
heal the pummeled heart,
the soul mired in sadness.
Comfort, comfort
all the divorced, the separated.
Enfold us in love.
Assure us of acceptance.
Amen.

NOTES
1. Dorothy Day, *The Long Loneliness,* excerpted in "Dorothy Day's Conversion," *St. Anthony Messenger,* November 1997, p. 12.

2. Dorothy Day, "Room for Christ," *Weavings,* Vol. XVIII, No. 5, Sept./Oct. 2003, p. 10.

3. Robert Van de Weyer, *Celtic Prayers* (Nashville, Tenn.: Abingdon Press, 1997), p. 33.

4. Ronald Rolheiser, *The Holy Longing* (New York: Doubleday, 1999), p. 194.

5. *Ibid.,* p. 195.

6. *Ibid.*

7. Josef Pieper, *Laughter: The Basis of Culture* (New York: New American Library, 1963), p. 40.

8. *Ibid.,* p. 41.

9. James Finley, *Merton's Palace of Nowhere* (Notre Dame, Ind.: Ave Maria Press, 1978), p. 115.

10. "Spring," *A Commentary on the Sonnets of G. M. Hopkins,* Peter Milward, S.J. (Chicago: Loyola University Press, 1969), p. 16.

Two

BE COMFORTED IN YOUR ANGER
A healing chapter for the justly irate

"ONE WHO IS SLOW TO ANGER IS BETTER THAN THE MIGHTY,
AND ONE WHOSE TEMPER IS CONTROLLED THAN ONE WHO
CAPTURES A CITY."
—PROVERBS 16:32

. . . . .

STORY TIME

The charismatic young celebrant was in the habit of making announcements just before the final blessing. However, this time he surprised the congregation by rising from the presider's chair and approaching the ambo with his head slightly bowed. There he unfolded a letter which he had been asked to read at every liturgy.

"I find this very difficult," he began, establishing eye contact with as many worshipers as he could. He made it clear that he was simply carrying out the instructions of the bishop as relayed to him by his pastor.

The embarrassment in his voice made even the post-liturgy parking lot sprinters edge back into their pews. Father George haltingly read the bishop's message about "a small number of priests in the diocese" who had been accused of sexual abuse of minors. The letter emphasized how few priests were involved in this scandalous behavior. It solicited the compassion and continuing support of the parishioners during this difficult time "for all of us."

Refolding the letter and lowering his head, the celebrant apologized for having to be the bearer of such discomforting news. As he left the ambo, the congregation applauded enthusiastically. A visitor in the parish, who was stunned by the contents of the letter, was equally shocked by the people's response.

Had they been so eager to relieve the celebrant's unease that they did not consider whether there were any victims of clerical abuse in the church that morning? Was their attention so riveted by the effect of the letter on its likeable reader that they had missed the horrendous message? Would not respectful silence or prayer for the victims and their abusers have been a more fitting response?

The visitor was still stewing over what he perceived as an exercise in duplicity when he picked up the Sunday paper at the market. There, in a front-page story, he discovered that the bishop had been involved in reassigning accused pedophiles without warning the parishes to which they were sent. The number of priests involved in the scandal was much higher than the few mentioned in the letter. And one of the accused, now retired, had previously served at the parish where the visitor had just participated in the liturgy.

As he read the details of how boys were seduced and betrayed, how their parents refused to believe their stories about Father X's indecent advances, how the abuse had crippled many emotionally and driven some to suicide, he heard himself cursing aloud. He recalled his own years in a Catholic boarding school. "If any of those perverts had made a move on me, I would have given him something to remember me by," he muttered.

The article went on but the man could stomach no more. He threw the paper on the floor, changed clothes, and began running down the street toward the park. A lifelong Catholic, he felt betrayed by those whose behavior should have been above reproach. Images of trusted priests preying on children drove him to run flat out, break a sweat, pray in spurts: "God, help us!"

When he finally collapsed on a park bench, he was drenched. His anger had cooled as his body overheated. He thought about particular priests who had befriended and inspired him over the years. Father Pat who assured him in confession that he was not going to hell for giving Michael Kelly a black eye in third grade. Father Angelo who prayed for him in high school when he thought he might have a vocation to the priesthood, and kept praying for him even when he decided that he did not. And Father Bob who had

. . . . .

"WE ARE APT TO SHUT OUR EYES AGAINST A PAINFUL TRUTH."
—Patrick Henry

. . . . .

"ANGER IS A SHORT MADNESS."
—Horace

. . . . .

counseled him through a broken relationship that might otherwise have embittered him.

"I've got to put this thing in perspective and decide what to do about it," he told himself, as he began walking home. Certainly he was not the only one who would be seeking an effective way to respond to the tragedy.

The one thing he knew he would not do is deny his outrage at the criminal behavior of some of the ordained in his own church. "If I don't speak out on this one, I'm an enabler," he told himself. Remembering Jesus with his improvised whip of cords in the temple, he prayed, "Show me what to do with my anger."

SCRIPTURAL VOICES

Anger at the unjust actions of others often inhabited the heart of the Rabbi from Nazareth. All four evangelists record how the patience of Jesus was repeatedly tried by some of the scribes and Pharisees who abused their authority as religious leaders and guides. They often failed to do what they required of others, laying legalistic burdens on them. Imposing the letter of the law, they were untrue to its spirit. And by their craving for status symbols and titles, they revealed their inner poverty.

What comfort can those of us who struggle with anger against injustice take from the witness of Christ himself? How can we learn to muster the inner resources he had at his command in times of conflict and contention?

A few briefly considered gospel scenes that may point the way:

(Scene One) When the Pharisees attempt to snare him into denying Caesar's right to collect taxes, Jesus immediately senses their malicious intent. He sees through their manipulative flattery and is not deterred from exposing it for what it is.

"Why are you putting me to the test, you hypocrites?" he asks. "Show me the coin used for the tax" (Matthew

. . . . .

"REASON OPPOSES EVIL ALL THE MORE EFFECTIVELY WHEN ANGER RESIDES AT HER SIDE."
—Pope Gregory the Great

. . . . .

22:18). Then, displaying the coin his opponents have obligingly produced, Jesus inquires whose head and title are displayed there. They aver that it is the emperor's.

Sharp as a sickle felling ripe wheat, Jesus amazes his opponents by instructing them to "Give therefore to the emperor the things that are the emperor's, and to God the things that are God's" (Matthew 22:21).

By this example, Jesus encourages us to give voice to our anger when we are certain of the truth we are upholding. He would not have us "make nice" or pretend that we do not recognize an authority figure's manipulation. Like him, we can enlist honesty and wit in the cause of raising another's awareness of reality. We can require respect by setting boundaries against duplicity.

(Scene Two) After his exultant entry into Jerusalem, Jesus shocks many who think they know him. Fashioning himself a whip, he storms through the temple, driving the dove-sellers and moneychangers before him like startled cattle, overturning their tables and taking charge with undaunted proprietorship. His voice betrays no fear as he says, "Is it not written, 'My house shall be called a house of prayer for all the nations'? But you have made it a den of robbers" (Mark 11:17).

Once again his zeal for the truth drives him to express his anger. The result is, as Mark goes on to tell us, the frightened chief priests and scribes "kept looking for a way to kill him" (11:18).

Christ's example is instructive to those who harbor anger against the unjust actions of religious and political leaders. Like him, we ask ourselves: Is our anger fully justified? Is it based on our love for God and our fellow human beings? Is it rooted in fidelity to God? Have we exhausted nonviolent channels of making the truth known? (Consider how often Jesus attempted to get through to the scribes and Pharisees before he took this dramatic action.)

> "TO DO GOOD FOR OTHERS... MAY MEAN TO STAND UP TO THEM, TO RESIST THE EVIL THEY DO TO THEMSELVES AND TO OTHERS."
> —E. Glenn Hinson

24

If these questions can be answered affirmatively, we may decide to take symbolic actions that give disciplined vent to our anger without harming any person. We choose such actions in the full knowledge that there may well be difficult consequences. When Philip Berrigan and other Plowshares activists hammered on nuclear submarines, they accepted the likelihood that they would wind up in jail. However, like Jesus in the temple, such impassioned peacemakers are certain of their call and courageously act on it.

Few of us would imagine finding comfort in incarceration. But for some who are guided by a mature conscience, there is consolation in activating their righteous anger despite the costs.

(*Scene Three*) As Matthew tells it, shortly after the cleansing of the temple, Jesus warns his disciples against the self-aggrandizement of religious leaders who crave authority over others. Knowing that his time is short, he then assaults the scribes and Pharisees with a volley of wounding "Woes!" All the pain their hypocrisy and hardheartedness has inflicted on him is packed into these seven accusations of infidelity to God. His anger is afire. His opponents can choose whether to be cleansed or condemned by it.

> Woe to you, scribes and Pharisees, hypocrites! For you tithe mint, dill and cummin, and have neglected the weightier matters of the law: justice and mercy and faith. It is these you ought to have practiced without neglecting the others. You blind guides! You strain out a gnat but swallow a camel! (Matthew 23:23–24)

They have denied every opportunity for conversion, denied him as the Messiah, denied in him the God they claim to honor. Jesus, who is himself the way, the truth, and the life, sees no alternative but to denounce their sinfulness with a

. . . . .

"GOD IS A RIGHTEOUS JUDGE, AND A GOD WHO HAS INDIGNATION EVERY DAY."
—Psalm 7:11

. . . . .

"THERE IS A HOLY ANGER, EXCITED BY ZEAL, THAT MOVES US TO REPROVE WITH WARMTH THOSE WHOM OUR MILDNESS FAILED TO CORRECT."
—Jean Baptiste de la Salle

. . . . .

fury that may strike its target. Perhaps a few of his opponents will discern the truth they have hidden from themselves.

The comfort to be gained from such an encounter bears no resemblance to a maternal embrace. It is the muscular consolation of the warrior who has acted with courage and corrective love.

Who has experienced this stern comfort? Every Christian who has harnessed his or her anger to the witness of Christ. Every Martin Luther King, Jr., known and unknown, who has confronted racism's rubber bullets and snarling police dogs. Every Joan Chittister, O.S.B., known and unknown, who has confronted injustice in the church. Every Oscar Romero, known and unknown, who has confronted oppression of the poor and disenfranchised. Every victim of abuse who has stood up and said, "Enough. No more."

To all who wonder whether they are called to hone their anger as a nonviolent weapon against injustice, the psalmist advises:

> Wait for the LORD;
> be strong, and let your heart take courage;
> wait for the LORD!" (Psalm 27:14)

SPIRITUAL KIN

For most of us, channeling righteous anger against large-scale injustices is not our primary problem with anger. The causes of our hostility are apt to be found much closer to home. Our adversaries may be occupying the next cubicle, the house next door, or even the same bedroom. We cannot escape the reality that often enough the people who populate our daily lives are our most reliable aggravators as well as our most certain spiritual directors. If we are never irked by a spouse's leaving the toilet seat up or the dirty dishes in the sink, if we are unfailingly patient when the preschoolers are bickering or the teens are hoodwinking us out of the car keys, then sanctity is merely a hair's breadth away.

However, for the rest of us, there are several degrees of anger yet to be mastered. The wise will seek comfort and counsel from those fifth-century elders collectively known as the Desert Fathers and Mothers.

In cameo appearances, these seers now point the way:

(*Cameo One*) Abbot Macarius, having observed us losing our cool while disciplining a child or reacting to a spouse's provocation, advises: "If, wishing to correct another, you are moved to anger, you gratify your own passion. Do not lose yourself in order to save another."[1]

How often have we felt the adrenaline rush of venting our irritation by chewing another out? Did we secretly enjoy that sense of our own superiority or our ability to intimidate another? Were we convinced that we were teaching or guiding when we were, in fact, indulging ourselves? We can take comfort in knowing that Macarius came by his advice honestly after learning to rein in his own anger at his imperfect brothers.

(*Cameo Two*) Abbot Anthony, having noted how we flare up at verbal affronts or impudence, comes to our aid by advising: "You, brother [or sister], are like a house with a big strong gate, that is freely entered by robbers through all the windows."[2]

Have others, whose opinion we trust, ever pointed out that we are too thin-skinned, too ready to detect an insult where none was intended? Are we adept at telling the difference between constructive criticism and verbal abuse? Might we be over-defending what we take to be our honor at the cost of gaining discernment about ourselves? We can take comfort in knowing that Anthony too grew wiser by practicing humility and patience in the face of insults, real and imagined.

(*Cameo Three*) Abbot Sisois, having seen how ready we are to lose our tempers over the inevitable setback that we are sure

. . . . .

"ANGER IS A TOOL FOR CHANGE WHEN IT CHALLENGES US TO BECOME MORE OF AN EXPERT ON THE SELF AND LESS OF AN EXPERT ON OTHERS."
—Harriet Lerner, Ph.D.

. . . . .

we do not deserve, counsels us: "Any evil that comes to you, confess that it has happened to you because of your sins, for you must learn to attribute everything to the dispensation of God's wisdom."[3]

Does this sound too harsh to us, as though God were clobbering us with tribulations in retribution for our sins? That cannot be Sisois' meaning, since Jesus assured his disciples that neither the blind man's nor his parents' sins were the cause of his trouble. (See John 9:1–3.)

Abbot Sisois's message to modern readers might be put this way: When something bad happens to you, remember that you are a sinner who deserves no fewer hardships than your brothers and sisters endure. What God will make of your suffering remains to be seen. All of us are notoriously inadequate at perceiving the larger picture in which our small lives are embedded. Patience is a clearer lens than anger.

(*Cameo Four*) Finally, a pungent sermon from the early Desert Father Evagrius Ponticus offers us instructive consolation. His advice for ascetics of his day holds true for all who seek to be liberated from the rattling chains of ruinous anger.

> We need to reclaim anger for its proper purpose. It is always a waste of good anger to get annoyed with other human beings.... What the ascetic needs to do is to focus his attention...on the fact that he is annoyed. Instead of seeing some other human being angrily, he tries to see his own anger. He can then begin to fight against it.[4]

As our self-knowledge increases, our compulsion to reprimand others decreases. The time we no longer waste in removing the specks from our neighbors' eyes can be invested in dislodging the log from our own.

. . . . .

"THE WISE [PERSON] FORGETS INSULTS AS THE UNGRATEFUL FORGET BENEFITS."
—Chinese proverb

. . . . .

"THE MORE YOU COMPLAIN, THE LONGER GOD LETS YOU LIVE."
—Russian proverb

. . . . .

CREATIVE WORKS

Unattended, anger can insinuate itself into every corner of our psychic house like cobwebs that no longer prompt removal. We may contentedly go on thinking of ourselves as good, church-going Christians who are occasionally provoked at those less virtuous than ourselves. If there are people with whom we are at odds, we put them out of our minds or cross the street when they head in our direction.

The masterful spiritual writer Henri J.M. Nouwen recognized this tendency to blindness in those of us who are upright servants of the Lord. In a short story called "Anger's Burden," Nouwen imagines himself encountering a stranger in the mirror. This aging, unkempt man bends Nouwen's ear with a turgid stream of complaints about all the injustices he has suffered.

The more the man gripes about everything that is wrong in the world, the more Nouwen feels a cold darkness enveloping him. He wants to speak up about the man's unrecognized blessings. He seems to be powerless before the deluge of negativity.

Later, away from the mirror, Nouwen envisions the stranger nearly bent to the ground, dragging an enormous burden behind him. The author realizes that the burden is made up of all those at whom the man is angry, against whom he holds resentment. Like Marley's ghost, he is condemned to haul his load wherever he goes.

As Nouwen gazes in pity at the vision, an inner voice informs him, "You are that man."[5] His eyes are reluctantly opened to how much a part of his identity that burden has become. He wonders how different he might be if he were divested of all those he has judged and condemned. Who would he be without his enemies? Without those to whom he feels morally superior?

The author realizes that he has been enlightened by an encounter with his angry self. He asks himself how this encounter will affect him in the years remaining to him.

. . . . .

"THE LONGER WE DWELL ON OUR MISFORTUNES, THE MORE POWER THEY HAVE TO HARM US."
—Voltaire

. . . . .

"If I die an angry man shackled to the burden of my past," he realizes, "I will be too heavy for the resurrection!"[6]

Washed clean by this sun-drenched truth, Nouwen hears a familiar voice that he has always loved: "Do not judge, and you will not be judged; do not condemn, and you will not be condemned. Forgive, and you will be forgiven" (Luke 6:37).

At this point, Jesus departs from the gospel script. He urges Nouwen to cut himself free from his self-imposed burden and realize how much he is loved as a child of God. Then anger will be evicted from his heart, and gratitude will make its dwelling there.

When Nouwen awakens, he makes peace with his angry self and thanks him for the illuminating visit. The "two" embrace, realizing their need to "always stay in touch."[7]

. . . . .

"NOT UNDERSTANDING WHAT HAS HAPPENED PREVENTS US FROM GOING ON TO SOMETHING BETTER."
—Abba Poeman

. . . . .

CONTEMPORARY WISDOM

Anger rarely fails to make an appearance on the front page. Terrorist threats. Wars rumbling on. Public officials denouncing others. Attorneys hurling javelin-charges. Racists, sexists or homophobes fouling the atmosphere. In this contentious age, we require mentors who recognize the roots of anger and are skilled at sowing peace. Among the many whose wisdom is ours for the asking are the Buddhist monk Thich Nhat Hanh and the Catholic Cardinal Joseph Bernardin.

Thich Nhat Hanh served as the chairman of the Vietnamese Buddhist Peace Delegation during the war. Since that time, he has become an internationally known teacher, poet and mentor of those who seek peace in their lives and in their world. Exiled from his own country, he lives in an ecumenical community at Plum Village in southwest France.

To profit from Nhat Hanh's teaching, the reader must go directly to works like *Being Peace* and *Going Home: Jesus and*

Buddha as Brothers. These books and his many others play variations on the simple theme of practicing mindfulness as a path to peace. The person who is faithful to daily breathing, sitting or walking meditations gradually comes to realize the consolation of being in touch with God at every moment.

However, Nhat Hanh is realistic enough to know that many of us try to evade our suffering by crawling under the comforter of distractions. Instead of touching God and our true selves, we clasp the remote control to escape from awareness. We cooperate in our own spiritual depletion.

Meditation moves us deeper into awareness of the reality of the present moment. It secures us from the illusions that manufacture psychic smog. It enables us to relax and smile. "A smile makes you master of yourself," Nhat Hanh insists. "It is with our capacity of smiling, breathing, and being peace that we can make peace."[8]

For those who are chronically angry, attention to that simple reality must be paid. If we bury our anger or deny its existence, we perpetuate its power to harm us and others. Nhat Hanh uses a memorable image to help us see the situation more clearly:

> Like a fireman, we have to pour water on the blaze first, and not waste time looking for the one who set the house on fire. Breathing in, I know that I am angry. Breathing out, I know that I must put all my energy into caring for my anger.[9]

Equally counterproductive is the habit of feeding our anger by blaming others for "making us mad." Instead of accepting responsibility for our reaction to another's provocation, we focus on the other as the uncontrollable culprit.

Thich Nhat Hanh teaches a process of recognizing the energy of anger that is in us, and embracing it so that it cannot cause harm. Through meditation and awareness, our

. . . . .

"YOUR ANGER DOES NOT PRODUCE GOD'S RIGHTEOUSNESS."
—James 1:20

. . . . .

"IF WE CANNOT FIND PEACE INSIDE OURSELVES, IT IS USELESS TO LOOK FOR IT ELSEWHERE."
—La Rochefoucauld

. . . . .

anger is given the opportunity to wane without negative consequences.

To his Christian retreatants, Nhat Hanh recommends asking Jesus to help them recognize and accept their anger. Prayer and scripture reflection aid the process of moving out of the danger zone where anger gives birth to resentment and revenge. "You are able to contain, to control, to transform the negative energy in you, the energy you call the evil spirit," the monk advises.[10]

When Cardinal Joseph Bernadin was accused of sexual abuse in 1993, the charges against him were widely publicized. He was overwhelmed by the horror of this unexpected suffering. "I was angry and bewildered that people who did not know me would make such destructive charges against me," he wrote.[11]

Knowing that he had to confront the young man who had accused him, Cardinal Bernardin went to meet Steven Cook. The accused had fortified himself with prayer and meditation. He calmly invited his accuser to tell his story.

In that peaceful atmosphere, the truth emerged. Steven Cook had been persuaded by an attorney and an unscrupulous priest to target Bernardin. Cook apologized to the cardinal, who had been praying for him daily. The young man explained that he had been alienated from the church since a seminary teacher abused him several years earlier. When Bernardin offered to celebrate Mass for him, Cook at first declined. He admitted that his anger at the church often moved him to throw the Bible against the wall.

But the cardinal was not deterred. He took out two gifts for Steven Cook. One was a Bible which he had inscribed to his accuser. The other was a century-old chalice given to Bernardin for the express purpose of saying Mass for this young man who was battling AIDS. In tears, Cook asked the cardinal to celebrate Mass then and there.

Recalling the event in his book *The Gift of Peace,* Joseph Bernardin described it as the most profound experience of

"EVERYTHING THAT IRRITATES US ABOUT OTHERS CAN LEAD TO AN UNDERSTANDING OF OURSELVES."
—Carl Jung

"NOTHING ON EARTH CONSUMES A [PERSON] MORE QUICKLY THAN THE PASSION OF RESENTMENT."
—Friedrich Nietzsche

peace and reconciliation he had ever had. "It was a manifestation of God's love, forgiveness, and healing that I will never forget," he wrote.[12]

The energy of anger in both the accused and the accuser was transformed into peace. Cardinal Bernardin and Steven Cook remained friends. When the older man was diagnosed with cancer six months later, the younger man wrote to console him. He planned to travel to Chicago to visit his new friend.

However, Steven Cook died before he could make that journey. The following autumn, on November 14, 1996, Joseph Cardinal Bernardin died. He had just completed his work on *The Gift of Peace*.

The Cardinal closes his book by inviting his readers to join him in offering the prayer attributed to Saint Francis of Assisi:

> Lord, make me an instrument of your peace.
> Where there is hatred, let me sow love.
> Where there is injury, pardon.
> Where there is doubt, faith.
> Where there is despair, hope.
> Where there is darkness, light.
> Where there is sadness, joy.
> O Divine Master, grant that I may not so
>   much seek
> to be consoled, as to console;
> to be understood, as to understand;
> to be loved, as to love;
> for it is in giving that we receive,
> it is in pardoning that we are pardoned.
> It is in dying that we are born to eternal life.

. . . . .

"ANY UNREST AND ANY STRIFE CAN BE BORNE IF WE FIND PEACE WHERE WE LIVE."
—Teresa of Avila

. . . . .

Together, Thich Nhat Hanh and Joseph Cardinal Bernardin invite us to be comforted in our anger by recognizing it, embracing it, inviting Jesus to transform it into the constructive, life-giving energy of peace. These two mentors are, like Jesus and Buddha, brothers who urge us to become instruments of peace in a contentious world.

HOLY LAUGHTER

If there is any more surefire dissipater of anger than laughter, I have yet to encounter it. It is the fire extinguisher ready at hand for the irate, the healing balm for the habitually fuming. As a recovering perfectionist who can hardly get through the day without bumping into some cause for vexation, I could not survive without holy laughter. Without my humor files, I would take to my bed, languishing like a Victorian maiden deprived of her smelling salts.

A friend—or an enemy—who can make me laugh at myself when I am exasperated is mending my spiritual well-being. For example: I once heatedly denounced an editor who had failed to give me the extra assignment he had promised to provide. The supplemental income would have allowed me to buy a totally superfluous DVD player. Waiting for my tirade to subside, a friend remarked, "But, Gloria, it's like Steven Wright says, you can't have everything. Where would you put it?" My anger and acquisitiveness quickly fled the scene.

Even as sober-sided a saint as John Chrysostom taught that "Laughter has been implanted in our soul that the soul may some time be refreshed." Saint Ignatius Loyola, brilliant founder of the Jesuits, taught young novices that, out of love for Jesus and gratitude for their blessings, they should be happy to be reckoned fools by the irreligious. "Laugh and grow strong," he counseled.

However, the patron saint of good humor should surely be Philip Neri. The sixteenth-century founder of the Congregation of the Oratory was famous in his day as a practical joker who often wandered the streets of Rome decked out in a jester's costume. He likewise indulged his sense of play by shaving his beard on one side only.

. . . . .

"WHEN YOU ARE DISTURBED, DO NOT SIN; PONDER IT ON YOUR BEDS, AND BE SILENT."
—Psalm 4:4–5

. . . . .

"LAUGHTER IS THE SOUND OF A SOUL WAKING UP."
—Hafiz

. . . . .

Philip, who was an excellent scholar and preacher, used humor for three basic purposes. The first was to dissuade people from raising him up on a pedestal as the admired "holy father." The second was to persuade self-righteous Christians not to take themselves too seriously. And the third was to balance life's suffering with equal time for good cheer.

When I recall how I once craved the austere penances of a primitive monastic order, I take pleasure in Philip Neri's advice to a novice. The young man requested permission to wear a hair shirt. To which his superior responded, "Yes, but wear it outside your clothes."

Or when I consider how I often want to be seen as a person of some importance, I recall Philip's advice to the young aristocrats of Rome. They came to him seeking spiritual guidance befitting their exalted social caste. He obliged by requiring them to walk his little dog on crowded city streets. As they departed leading the dog, he corrected them, saying, "No, no. You walk, but carry the dog."

On a day when anger threatens to get the better of me, I can always call on Philip Neri to come to the rescue. He reiterates his motto, "A joke a day and I am on my way with no care about tomorrow." And if my anger happens to be directed at the powers that be in church or state, I remember Philip's insistence to the Oratorians that "If you want to be obeyed, don't give commands."

This cheerful saint's humor sprang like sunflowers from the good soil of his humility. When he fasted from self-importance and religious scrupulosity, he knew enough to do so with a smile. And when anger threatened to derail him, he was always ready to draw the rubber sword of ready laughter.

. . . . .

"HE DESERVES PARADISE WHO MAKES HIS COMPANIONS LAUGH."
—the Qur'an

. . . . .

REFLECT

In what ways will you attempt to harness your justified anger to prayer and reason?

Be Comforted

How will you seek comfort in the teachings of Jesus and others in this chapter as you examine the causes of your anger?

PRAY
O Divine Comforter,
cool the angry heart,
the soul battered by injustice.
Comfort, comfort
all who contend against evil.
Harness our passion.
Cleanse us of hate.
Amen.

NOTES

1. Thomas Merton, *The Wisdom of the Desert* (New York: New Directions, 1960), p. 31.

2. *Ibid.*, p. 46.

3. *Ibid.*, p. 38.

4. Ernest Kurtz and Katherine Ketcham, *The Spirituality of Imperfection: Storytelling and the Journey to Wholeness* (New York: Bantam Books, 1992), p. 214.

5. Henri J. M. Nouwen, "Anger's Burden," *Weavings*, Vol. IX, No. 2, March/April 1994, p. 28.

6. *Ibid.*, p. 28.

7. *Ibid.*, p 30.

8. Thich Nhat Hanh, *Being Peace* (Berkeley, CA: Parallax Press, 1987), pp. 6, 9.

9. Thich Nhat Hanh, "Peace Is Every Step," *Parabola*, Vol. XVI, No. 4, p. 73, quoted in "Anger: An Instrument of Peace," by C. Gordan Peerman, III, *Weavings*, Vol. IX, No. 2, March/April 1994, p. 18.

10. Thich Nhat Hanh, *Going Home: Jesus and Buddha As Brothers* (New York: Riverhead Books, 1999), p. 194.

11. Joseph Cardinal Bernardin, *The Gift of Peace: Personal Reflections* (Chicago: Loyola Press, 1997), p. 24.

12. *Ibid.*, p. 39.

Three

BE COMFORTED IN YOUR ANXIETY
A healing chapter for the fearful

"BANISH ALL ANXIETY FROM YOUR MIND."
—ECCLESIASTES 11:10

. . . . .

STORY TIME

Hearing herself described as a widow, she still felt mistakenly identified although Jack's heart attack had come six months ago. Their two grown children lived in distant states with their own families. Keeping the house seemed like a good idea, at least until she retired. "That will be soon enough to get an apartment closer to Karen or Brian," she thought.

The widow felt fairly secure. As an editor, she had long been employed by a Catholic publisher. She enjoyed the privilege of working out of her home office. After Jack's death, her weekly deadlines became therapeutic. "Thank God for my work," she thought. "I'd be lost without it."

When the phone rang on a clear June day, Marge was surprised to hear the voice of the general manager. As they exchanged pleasantries, she wondered if the publishing house was planning some sort of celebration to which she was about to be invited. Once or twice a year she was required to travel to Chicago for editorial meetings. However, it was the editorial director who called her on those occasions.

"I'm sorry to be the one who has to tell you, Marge, that your services will no longer be required after the end of the month. A new management team is taking over and there will be no more home-office people on the staff," the general manager said, without changing his pleasant tone.

There were additional remarks about the poor economy, wishes that things were different, thanks for her contributions to the company. Marge was unable to sort them out. Her brain had shut down. Or was it her hearing? Later she could not remember a word she had said. However, it crossed her mind that she might have thanked him for calling to tell her personally that she was being permanently laid off.

"What was I thinking of?" she asked, when she came to herself. "I should have asked him if this was the best they could do after twenty-four years of service. He didn't even offer me a severance package. Just dumped me like some trash."

Although the general manager had gone to great lengths to insist that there was nothing personal in Marge's dismissal, she felt no less rejected. The possibility of not keeping her job until she was old enough to retire with full benefits had not crossed her mind. In her naiveté, she had assumed that a publisher of religious books would not be so shackled to the bottom line that they would lop off their over-sixty employees like dead branches.

. . . . .

"GOD WANTS US TO KNOW THAT HE KEEPS US SAFE THROUGH GOOD AND ILL."
—Julian of Norwich

. . . . .

After the fire of anger came the ashes of anxiety. Within two short weeks, there would be no more direct deposit paychecks in her modest account. Should she apply for social security now even though she would barely have enough to live on? What about health insurance? Prescription costs? If the coming New England winter were as harsh as the last one, would she be able to cover the fuel bills? How should she try to supplement Jack's social security checks?

Her fears were the worst of noisy neighbors, keeping her awake long after midnight. "What ifs?" hounded her. She knew there were decisions to be made, steps to be taken, survival techniques to be learned.

Marge made a list of things to do. But the woman who had been a paragon of productivity now found herself unable to stick with the tasks at hand. Each time she completed one item on the list (a job application or an entry on her employment security work log), she rewarded herself with a few games of Free Cell on the computer or simply took a "nap" during which she rested her body while worrying in a more concentrated manner. Then she got up again and took refuge in what she thought of as mindless housework. She felt as though she were walking around under a bearskin rug with the bear still in it.

Of course Marge prayed for relief from the daily round of worry. But she barely believed in the possibility of the relief she sought. Fear of an uncertain future accompanied her throughout the day like a muffled radio station that causes rather than quiets discontent.

Only when desperation overtook anxiety did she call her pastor. As a parishioner, Marge had always been a provider of services: catechist, lector and soup kitchen volunteer. "Now I'm the one who's begging for help," she thought, recoiling from her own neediness. When Father Bertram answered, she said, without introduction, "I've lost my job. I don't know how to handle it. Do you have time to see me?"

Her voice betrayed her condition. Father Bertram responded, "Absolutely, Marge. Let me rearrange a few things and you can come in this afternoon. How about three o'clock? We'll talk it over and see what needs to be done."

She put the phone down, caught her breath. The comfort she had always felt in sharing her worries with Jack returned. Marge gave herself permission to lean on Father Bertram. He was a good man, at-home with his priesthood.

The widow poured a cup of coffee and stretched her legs under the kitchen table. For the first time since her termination, she felt a slow infusion of confidence. Out of nowhere, a quip from Mark Twain flitted across her memory like a firefly. "I have worried about many things in my life. But most of them never happened." She laughed in recognition.

SCRIPTURAL VOICES

From Genesis to Revelation, the Lord can scarcely take a break from his responsibilities as the Alleviator of Anxiety. "Do not be afraid," he says to the heirless Abraham, soothing his worries about Sarah's infertility (Genesis 15:1). And "Do not be afraid," Christ says to John as the Son of Man

. . . . .

"TO THE CHEROKEE, WORRY IS THE *DELALA*, THE WOODPECKER, PECKING AWAY ON THE ROOF."
—Joyce Sequichie Hifler

. . . . .

"THE WAY OF FAITH IS NECESSARILY OBSCURE. WE DRIVE BY NIGHT."
—Thomas Merton

. . . . .

appears bearing stars in his hand and wielding a sharp sword between his teeth (Revelation 1:17).

Those comforting "fear nots" are addressed to Mary at the Annunciation and to Joseph as he frets over his espoused's pregnancy; to Zechariah and to the shepherds as they are separately confronted by angels; to Simon who was knocked to his knees by the awesome power of the Fisher of Men, and to Jairus, when the frightened father thought his daughter was dead; to Mary Magdalene and "the other Mary" who clutched the glowing feet of the just-risen Lord. Those two sustaining words are addressed to disciples and other believers at times of crisis when fear is the deluge that would sweep them out to sea.

For Americans, crisis is defined by the events of September 11, 2001, when death descended out of a clear blue sky. The terror that took us by the throat and shook us did not soon leave us. Over the ensuing weeks it retracted its claws and slunk around under the guise of habitual anxiety. It has yet to depart from many hearts. We are victims of a poker-faced uncertainty that rarely takes a day off.

As a Russian artist observed, "Until September 11, America had been the only place in the world where one could live without fear." We ask ourselves: How would Jesus respond to that remark? Are we and our children sentenced without bail to the lock-up of fear and anxiety? Did the terrorists get away with our peace of mind?

When Jesus was about to send out the twelve "like sheep into the midst of wolves," he warned them that they must be "wise as serpents and innocent as doves" (Matthew 10:16). He told them straight out that they could expect to be harassed and persecuted. Should they be put on trial for their witness to him, they were not to worry. The Spirit, their invincible Advocate and Comforter, would speak through them.

Jesus then offered his friends a solace which they could not immediately grasp. He told them:

> "THAT THE BIRDS OF WORRY AND CARE FLY ABOUT YOUR HEAD, THIS YOU CANNOT CHANGE. BUT THAT THEY BUILD NESTS IN YOUR HAIR, THIS YOU CAN PREVENT."
> —Chinese proverb

So have no fear of them; for nothing is
covered up that will not be uncovered,
and nothing secret that will not become
known. What I say to you in the dark, tell
in the light; and what you hear whispered, proclaim from the housetops. Do
not fear those who kill the body but cannot kill the soul; rather fear him who can
destroy both soul and body in hell.
(Matthew 10:26–28)

At the time, the Good News of the reign of God was still
like a secret no more than whispered among the compara-
tive few who had encountered Christ. The only force that
could prevent the wider proclamation of Jesus' teaching was
fear itself. If the disciples cowered before their persecutors,
they would place their souls in jeopardy.

Jesus surely knew how hard it would be for his followers to entrust their lives, as he had, to the Father. So he rallied them by asking:

Are not two sparrows sold for a penny?
Yet not one of them will fall to the ground
apart from your Father. And even the
hairs of your head are all counted. So do
not be afraid; you are of more value than
many sparrows. (Matthew 10:29–31)

He understood their fear, knew they had just cause for anxiety, but affirmed their ability to go beyond it. If they could
not trust the Father, who cherished every hair and counted
every tear, what meaning would their faith have? Even if
their enemies had the power to kill the body, what did it
matter? The Father had the power to raise them up to a state
where no enemy could touch them, where there could, in
truth, be no enemies because all would be one in him.

Just as Jesus did not allow himself to be ruled by fear of
those who threatened his life, he urges those he loves not to

. . . . .

"I SOUGHT THE
LORD, AND HE
ANSWERED ME,
AND DELIVERED
ME FROM ALL MY
FEARS."
—Psalm 34:4

. . . . .

"THE POWER OF
CHRIST'S CROSS
AND
RESURRECTION IS
GREATER
THAN ANY EVIL
WHICH MAN
COULD OR
SHOULD FEAR."
—Pope John
Paul II

. . . . .

accommodate anxiety over terrorism. "And can any of you by worrying add a single hour to your span of life?" (Matthew 6:27). It is wise to provide as well as we can for our own and others' security. Yet it is wiser to spend our energies not in fretting but in coming to terms with the causes of terrorism, and in working for peace in whatever ways lie open to us. While we are praying and working for an end to enmity, we will have little time to worry about the latest Homeland Security color code.

"So do not worry about tomorrow," Jesus advises, "for tomorrow will bring worries of its own. Today's trouble is enough for today" (Matthew 6:34).

CREATION/CREATIVE WORKS

Stress is a cat burglar who makes off with our senses. Anyone who has ever had to appear in court, give a public speech, keep vigil over a feverish child, or interview for a crucial job has been victimized by it. Anyone who has ever had to go to war, to prison or into a burning building can recount the nightmares stress has scripted for their ongoing distress.

A case in point: When Rosa had to testify in court against her neighbor's abusive husband, she was besotted by nervousness. At the pretrial meeting with her neighbor's attorney, she regretted ever agreeing to testify. The defendant had never actually threatened her. But he had given her some menacing looks that said, "Stay out of this."

Now the attorney was questioning her about how she might respond to cross-examination. She understood only that he was asking her something. But his words sounded nonsensical. She could not identify whatever language he was using. Rosa simply stared at him. "What?" she asked, staring hard into his face in an attempt to read his expression.

The attorney repeated his last question, being careful not to signal that he was worried about the state of her mind. She was slightly dizzy. Her heart raced. "Why don't you take a few minutes and get some fresh air?" This time

"DO NOT FORGET YOUR PURPOSE AND DESTINY AS GOD'S CREATURE."
—Francis of Assisi

. . . . .

"FEAR NOT THAT YOUR LIFE WILL COME TO AN END, FEAR RATHER THAT IT WILL NEVER COME TO A BEGINNING."
—John Henry Newman

she understood the question and nodded. He stood and took her arm, perhaps thinking that her eyesight was also impaired.

Rosa welcomed the reprieve, thinking that if she did not feel better outside she would go to her car and leave. They would have to proceed without her testimony. Her companion led her to an enclosed courtyard. "I'll be back in about ten minutes," he said. "Don't worry. You'll do fine."

She sat down on a stone bench and took a series of deep breaths. The flow of fresh air through her nostrils worked like a tonic. She closed her eyes, concentrating on breathing in, breathing out. "Peace in," she recited silently as she inhaled. "Stress out" as she exhaled. Her heart began to settle into its accustomed pace. Rosa looked around at the unexpected Eden in which she found herself.

In the center of the courtyard was a small pond with a fountain. Its splashing came from another, more serene world. Two scarlet tropical fish drifted in their placid domain. They sailed gracefully through reflected lilies and irises, completely at their ease, untouched by the daily drama that embroiled others so close at hand.

Rosa breathed in the aroma of lilies, the self-assurance of the showy rhododendrons bordering the courtyard. A chickadee's outspoken call alerted her to the reality that others shared this sacred space. The peace of the courtyard flowed into her permeable body. She remembered the closing stanza of a poem by Mary Oliver:

> Never in my life
> had I felt myself so near
> that porous line
> where my own body was done with
> and the roots and the stems and the flowers
> began.[1]

The voices of the courtyard and the poet were joined by another in a three-part harmony. "Peace!" it said, "Be still!"

. . . . .

"Never be afraid to trust an unknown future to a known God."
—Corrie ten Boom

. . . . .

"Anxiety weighs down the human heart, but a good word cheers it up."
—Proverbs 12:25

. . . . .

(Mark 4:39). This voice brooked no nonsense about storms, agitations, unbridled stresses that threatened to swamp the boat. Rosa knew the voice of the Wind Tamer and Storm Queller. She blushed when he asked, "Why are you afraid? Have you still no faith?" (Mark 4:40). "Not as much as I thought," she replied. "Sorry."

When the attorney called to her from the doorway, he was instantly relieved. Her body was no longer hunched in a defensive posture, her face no longer pinched by stress. "Feeling better?" he asked, knowing the answer.

Rosa smiled, lifting her chin a bit like a boxer whom the odds favor. As they walked toward the courtroom, she wondered if her companion could smell the lilies that saturated her skin and hear the fountain splashing in easy laughter.

Much later, after the trial had gone as well as it needed to, Rosa bought a miniature fountain for her prayer table. "All you have to do is pour water into the container, plug it in, and enjoy the show," the clerk assured her. She placed six red carnations from the supermarket in a white vase by the fountain, adding sea glass and shells to the stones ringing the fountain's rim. Pulling the collected poems of Mary Oliver and the essays of Annie Dillard from her bookshelves, she arranged them like bowls of soul food on the white tablecloth. Then, lighting a candle at either side of the fountain, she sat back on her heels and said, "There."

If a sign were needed, it would have read, "Serenity Place. No stress allowed." It would always be there, calling her to stop, breathe, listen, pray. God would never allow her to be burdened beyond her strength. His yoke was easy. This haven was a reminder of the divine pledge. As for her half of the covenant, Rosa resolved that her prayer would rise like the fountain's graceful spray in daily fidelity.

CONTEMPORARY WISDOM
She dispenses her wisdom through stories like a sagacious

> . . . . .
> "IS NOT ONE REAL AIM OF SACRAMENT AND ART [POETRY] AN INNER CHANGE IN THE PARTICIPANT?"
> —John Savant
>
> . . . . .
> "GAZE AT THE BEAUTY OF EARTH'S GREENINGS."
> —Hildegard of Bingen
>
> . . . . .

grandmother who knows that if you do not need this particular story today, you will some day. Unlike the archetypical grandmother, however, Rachel Naomi Remen, M.D., draws from a larger and deeper well than most of us can access. She is a physician, a teacher, a therapist, and a person who has long coped with chronic illness. Her work with the Commonweal Cancer Help Program has placed her in privileged contact with those who suffer. As she contributes to her patient's comfort, they contribute to her wisdom. And she shares what she has gathered by writing books like *My Grandfather's Blessings* and *Kitchen Table Wisdom*.

Anxiety and fear of the unknown come with the territory of serious illness occupied by Rachel Remen's patients. She responds to them not only with medical knowledge but also with the life lessons she gained from her grandfather. Meyer Ziskind was an Orthodox rabbi and scholar of the kabbalah. More importantly to Rachel, he was the trusted source of religious wisdom to whom she always turned in her childhood.

As an accomplished worrier who began practicing in early childhood, I was especially comforted by one of Rachel Remen's stories entitled "What If God Blinks?" In it, she recalls an incident from her public school elementary days. The principal happened to be a fundamentalist Christian. At an assembly, the principal instructed the children that they should always kneel and pray three times a day. If they failed to do so, God might forget that they were there.

Although the adult Rachel cannot remember the principal's exact words, she has never forgotten the demonstration that accompanied the lesson. When a child failed to pray, God would turn his face away. And if that happened, "you would wither up and die, like an autumn leaf."[2] At that point, the speaker exhibited a large dead leaf to show the children what would become of them.

Five-year-old Rachel Remen immediately began to worry about the times between her thrice-daily prayers.

. . . . .

"I'M SIMPLY
TRYING TO
CONJURE UP
STORIES IN
WHICH PEOPLE
ARE TOUCHED
WITH WHAT MAY
OR MAY NOT BE
THE PRESENCE OF
GOD..."
—Frederick
Buechner

. . . . .

"[God] might blink and then what would become of me?" she wondered. So, in tears and trembling, she consulted her grandfather.

Stroking her hair, the rabbi asked his granddaughter if she were to wake up in the middle of the night, would she know that her parents were in the house with her. Rachel nodded that she would. He then asked how she would know of their presence. Would she hear them, see them, touch them?

With each new question, the child's tears lessened. She realized that she would simply know that she was not alone. Her grandfather was delighted. "Good! Good! That's how God knows you're there. He doesn't need to look at you to know that you are there. He just knows. In just the same way you know that God is there. You just know that He is there and you're not alone in the house."[3]

How often do we all, at five or thirty-five or seventy-five, need to be reassured that God is there and we are not alone in the house? Anxiety readily blinds us to his presence. Worry convinces us that we have no one to turn to in our trials. We need stories like this one to stroke our hair and call us back to reality.

Whenever I hear myself fretting over whether to pay exorbitant fees for health insurance or risk going without it, over whether losing my balance or having headaches could mean that I have cancer again, or whether I might wind up totally alone in my not-too-distant old age, I try to consult stories like this one. It's just what the doctor ordered. I realize that I can choose not to worry. Even if God does blink, he never leaves the room.

> "LET NOTHING DISTURB YOU, LET NOTHING FRIGHTEN YOU; ALL THINGS ARE PASSING; GOD NEVER CHANGES."
> —Teresa of Avila

HOLY LAUGHTER

Several years ago I read that a Florida bishop had suggested a fifth mark of the church. To "one, holy, catholic, and apostolic," he wanted to add "humorous." His point was that Catholics in the United States had matured to the point where they no longer needed to adopt a stern-faced defensive posture.

During those historic eras when immigrant Catholics had been persecuted or treated as a servile class, they had good reason to be sober about their public image. But, the Florida bishop believed, the presidency of John F. Kennedy and the rise of the educated Catholic middle class had propelled us to a new plateau. Now we should be confident enough to laugh at ourselves rather than hiding our foibles from public view. The bishop insisted that such levity was a sign of holiness.

G.K. Chesterton would second the bishop's motion. The witty author of the Father Brown mysteries, as well as numerous essays and poems, Chesterton held that laughter was a blessing to be enjoyed as often as possible. He observed: "A good joke is the one ultimate and sacred thing which cannot be criticized. Our relations with a good joke are direct and even divine relations."[4]

More familiar to us is Chesterton's remark that angels can fly "because they take themselves lightly." As we smile at this apparently artless aside, we realize that Chesterton was reminding us of another closer-to-home category of beings who wear life more like butterfly wings than a Puritan's wool cloak.

If, whenever we are weighted with worry, we were to find the nearest group of small children and watch them at play, might we remember the words of our Teacher? "Whoever does not receive the kingdom of God as a little child will never enter it" (Mark 10:15).

When Jesus so instructed his disciples, they were so absorbed with their own importance that they pompously dictated to women and children who were magnetized by the Lord. Mark notes that they "spoke sternly" to these little ones who wanted only to get close to Jesus.

In essence, the Rabbi told his companions, "Lighten up." We need not be anxious on his account. He is at home

. . . . .

"CAST ALL YOUR ANXIETY ON HIM, BECAUSE HE CARES FOR YOU."
—1 Peter 5:7

. . . . .

"WHAT IS THE WORK OF A SPIRITUAL MASTER? TO TEACH PEOPLE TO LAUGH."
—Anthony de Mello, S.J.

. . . . .

with children and angels, as well as with all who seek him for any reason.

Here is a comforting antidote I have relied on in times of high anxiety: Set aside fifteen minutes a day as your play-time. Resolve to entertain no worries during this brief time to be given without reserve to holy leisure and laughter. Gather resources that draw out the child within. Good jokes. Anecdotes about your own and others' children and grandchildren. Mandala coloring books and fine-line markers. Play-Doh or clay. Collections of columns by Erma Bombeck. Scenic or humorous puzzles of no more than a few hundred pieces. Whatever invites you to be at your ease in the presence of the Lord of Laughter.

Begin and end your playtime with extemporaneous prayer. Or recite the proverbs:

> "A cheerful heart is a good medicine,
>   but a downcast spirit dries up the bones."
> (Proverbs 17:22)

> "A glad heart makes a cheerful countenance,
>   but by sorrow of heart the spirit is broken."
> (Proverbs 15:13)

In my own campaign against anxiety, I have built up an armory of comic videos. I see in them not merely a few hours of escapist relief, but a gift from the Spirit of Wisdom who played before the Lord at the "beginning of his work." I am lifted out of my cares by the creative work of those whose calling is to give others cause for therapeutic laughter.

Find the comedies that work best for you, gather them close at hand, and thank God that it will be impossible to be worried while responding to the tribulations of characters who exist to amuse and painlessly instruct us. As Will Rogers observed, "Everything is funny as long as it is happening to somebody else."

Whatever troubles are feeding our anxieties, it is most likely that our favorite comic characters have managed to

. . . . .

"HOW COULD
JESUS HAVE
MANAGED TO
ATTRACT
CHILDREN,
WOMEN,
SIMPLE PEOPLE, IF
HE WAS ALWAYS
ALOOF AND
SERIOUS?"
—Jean Leclercq

. . . . .

triumph over greater ones. Picture Bruce Almighty overcoming job loss, domestic estrangement and utter failure at
being God's stand-in. Likewise, we can always take refuge in
comedy because a happy ending is guaranteed.

REFLECT

Who or what are the "usual suspects" when it comes to identifying the sources of your chronic worries or anxieties?
How will you apply at least one of the suggested sources of
comfort?

What specific practices are you willing to undertake as you
place greater trust in God's care for you?

PRAY

O Divine Comforter,
steady the anxious heart,
the soul deflated by fear.
Comfort, comfort,
all the worried and careworn.
Enlarge our confidence.
Empower us to walk on troubled
waters.
Amen.

. . . . .

"IF YOU DON'T
LEARN TO LAUGH
AT TROUBLE, YOU
WON'T HAVE
ANYTHING TO
LAUGH AT WHEN
YOU'RE OLD."
—Ed Howe

. . . . .

NOTES

1. "White Flowers," *New and Selected Poems*, Mary Oliver (Boston: Beacon Press, 1992), p. 59.

2. Rachel Naomi Remen, M.D., *Kitchen Table Wisdom* (New York: Riverhead Books, 1996), p. 263.

3. *Ibid.*, p. 265.

4. G. K. Chesterton, *Preface to Dickens, Pickwick Papers*. Bartlett's Familiar Quotations, ed. John Bartlett. Justin Kaplan, general editor. (Boston: Little, Brown and Company, 1992), p. 619.

Four

Be Comforted in Your Loneliness
A healing chapter for those who are alone

. . . . .

"Turn to me and be gracious to me,
for I am lonely and afflicted."
—Psalm 25:16

. . . . .

Story Time

While waiting in the supermarket checkout line, Frank glanced at the glossy magazine covers. A feature headline in *Redbook* caught his eye: "Why Settle for Loneliness?" it boldly inquired. Although the question was vitally important to him, Frank did not think a magazine would help.

At thirty-five he had never been married. Unlike many men of his age, he did not fear commitment nor did he shy away from the expenses of raising a family. He told himself he simply had no luck with women. His reflection in the mirror was inconclusive. It was true that his brown hair was a bit thin, his belt size larger than he would like. "But there are plenty of guys who look a lot worse than me who somehow got married," he told himself as he walked out of the store.

On the drive home he tortured himself by noticing all the couples on the street, imagining where they might be going for the evening. He felt separated from them by a wall that prevented the lonely from inhabiting the world of those who belonged to each other. The weekend stretched before him like a highway into the desert. His fishing buddy was away with his family. Frank would be alone, as he so often was on weekends.

Dinner was a tray of microwave macaroni and cheese. When he wanted to comfort himself with a cereal bowl of Ben and Jerry's "Chunky Monkey," he found a near-empty container in the freezer. Angrily, he threw it into the trashcan. "Do those guys who have wives have any idea how lucky they are?" he wondered. Even a microwave dinner would be a feast, Frank thought, if he had someone to share the meal with him.

"Lord, I'm not asking for much!" he complained. "Why is something that is so easy for everyone else so impossible for me? I can't stand to be alone all my life. You've got to help me."

He did not expect an answer. Picking up the remote, he sprawled on the couch and went through the motions of channel surfing. Bruce Springsteen's "57 Channels (And Nothin' On)" ran through his brain in a mocking tone. Desperation gnawed. He thought about calling Sarah, a coworker. "Yeah, right," he fretted, "Last time I called her she gave me some line about having to visit her grandmother. Like I'd believe that one."

However, after a half-hour of flicking from one inane sitcom to another, Frank was sinking in quicksand. He knew that if he did not take action, he would be immobilized until Monday morning. "God, let her be home. Let her say yes just this once. Help me out here."

It was the prayer of a man on a limb, a solitary owl's painful hoot. The phone slid in his sweaty palm. After three rings, Sarah's "Hello" shocked him. He forced himself to speak casually, as though it had just occurred to him that she might like to take in a last-minute movie. Apologizing for his lack of planning, he awaited his sentence.

"That sounds great," she said. "I was about to clean out my closets for lack of something better to do. Pick me up around seven, OK?"

"No problem," he replied. "See you then."

Frank headed for the shower, but stopped abruptly and glanced in the mirror again. He saw a man who was thankful that God had rescued him from a dark pit. On this one night he would not be alone. He realized, however, that his real need was to learn how to be alone without being laid low by alienation.

Sarah too lived alone. Maybe he would have the courage to ask her how she dealt with it. Maybe. But either way, tomorrow he would return to the supermarket. "I'm

. . . . .

"ALL THE LONELY PEOPLE, WHERE DO THEY ALL COME FROM?"
—John Lennon & Paul McCartney

. . . . .

"MAN IS THE ONLY BEING WHO FEELS HIMSELF ALONE AND THE ONLY ONE WHO IS SEARCHING FOR THE OTHER."
—Octavio Paz

. . . . .

man enough," he told himself. In the shower, he sang "57 Channels (And Nothin' On)" so raucously that his neighbor banged on the bathroom wall. Frank laughed out loud.

SCRIPTURAL VOICES

The most painful cries in the entire Bible come from Job, that sore-covered solitary seated on a dung heap. The sufferings of Job are so manifold and his innocence so manifest that his story appeals to all of us. We, too, have asked "Why?" or "Why me?" We too have had to bear the reality that no reason we can grasp will be given.

At the beginning of this poetic folk tale, Job is a chieftain surrounded by family, friends and herds of livestock. But once God gives Satan permission to test Job, our hero is left childless and herdless. His wife advises him to "Curse God and die" (2:9).

Job's loneliness on his island of suffering is intensified by the counterfeit comfort of his three friends (Eliphaz, Bildad and Zophar). They insist that he has deserved his plight through his unacknowledged sinfulness. They refute his protestations of blamelessness.

"I have heard many such things; miserable comforters are you all!" Job responds (16:2). He feels that God has not only forsaken him but also made him a target of divine wrath. Unattended and without relief of any kind, he protests:

> He has put my family far from me,
>> and my acquaintances are wholly estranged
>> from me.
> My relatives and my close friends have failed
> me;
>> the guests in my house have forgotten me;
> my serving girls count me as a stranger;
>> I have become an alien in their eyes.
> (Job 19:13–15)

. . . . .

"AND THE DAY CAME WHEN THE RISK TO REMAIN TIGHT IN A BUD WAS MORE PAINFUL...THAN THE RISK IT TOOK TO BLOSSOM."
—Anaïs Nin

. . . . .

"LONELINESS IS WHEN YOU'RE MISSING PEOPLE, ALONENESS IS WHEN YOU'RE ENJOYING YOURSELF."
—Anthony de Mello

. . . . .

However great his pain and deprivation, Job refuses to curse God or to retract his claim to innocence. He is completely alone. Yet he does not decide to take his own life. As he sums up his cause before his accusers, he plaintively recalls the good life he once knew.

Job pines for the days when his children were "round about" him, the elders and chiefs "listened and waited" for his counsel, the mourners "took comfort" from his cheerful presence, the poor and the needy "cried out" for his help (29:5–16).

Overcome by these memories of his former sense of belonging and acceptability, Job now sees himself as "a brother of jackals, and a companion of the ostriches" (30:29). After listening to the long-winded charges of Elihu, the young accuser with all the false answers, Job surely wishes he was beyond the range of any human voice.

However, that beleaguered victim then hears the one voice that can shatter his solitude. "Who is this that darkens counsel by words without knowledge?" the Lord inquires (38:2). And when the voice has forcefully reminded Job that the Almighty alone is God ("Shall a faultfinder contend with the Almighty?" [40:2]), Job readily bows to a greater wisdom.

Although God does not respond directly to Job's questions about his suffering, he is assured of the Almighty's awareness of him. The victim admits his own limited understanding of God's designs. He concludes: "[T]herefore I despise myself, / and repent in dust and ashes" (42:6).

Job's faith and integrity are then richly rewarded after he prays that his false friends will be spared the punishment they have earned. His brothers, sisters and former companions return to dine at his table. He and his wife produce seven sons and three daughters.

The wisdom Job had gained during his solitary confinement stood him in good stead. At a time when only sons inherited their father's wealth, Job bestowed on his beauti-

. . . . .

"I LIE AWAKE;
I AM LIKE A
LONELY BIRD ON
THE HOUSETOP."
—Psalm 102:7

. . . . .

"I AM A LONE
LORN CREETUR
. . . AND
EVERYTHINK
GOES
CONTRAIRY
WITH ME."
—Charles
Dickens

. . . . .

ful daughters "an inheritance among their brethren" (epilogue 15). And he lived to coddle his great-grandchildren.

CREATIVE WORKS

If loneliness were not so universal a suffering, the work of poets, musicians and filmmakers would be immeasurably depleted. Wordsworth might never have given us "I Wandered Lonely as a Cloud." Roy Orbison might never have crooned "Only the Lonely." Love makes the world go around. But the lack of it does a booming business as well.

Loneliness is as false an advisor as Eliphaz, Bildad and Zophar. It convinces us that we are worthless or undesirable. With little effort, it persuades us that all those happy couples in the commercials represent a reality from which we are alienated. In no time at all, it has us believing that we can never be content without a partner, friends, a group to rescue us from isolation.

In our saner moments, we know better. However, just as the wise do not wait to make out a will on their deathbeds, they prepare themselves in those saner moments for unexpected bouts of loneliness.

One way to do so is to mine the resources of poetry, music and film, seeking the particular works that will comfort us in our disconnection. We will often be rewarded with more than a temporary consolation.

Two Catholic poets who have served me well as guides through the fog of loneliness are the Jesuit Gerard Manley Hopkins and Carmelite Jessica Powers. His is the light to follow through the thickest darkness; hers is more fitting for those short spells of isolation that recur like showers in a New England April.

Hopkins (1844–1889) could no more have avoided loneliness than a poor Irish immigrant of his era could sidestep intolerance in Boston. He had a singular personality that set him apart from his fellow seminarians who enjoyed mocking his eccentric eloquence. His conversion to Catholicism in 1866 had riled his family and offended some

. . . . .

"FOR MY THOUGHTS ARE NOT YOUR THOUGHTS, NOR ARE YOUR WAYS MY WAYS, SAYS THE LORD."
—Isaiah 55:8

. . . . .

"HOW VERY GOOD AND PLEASANT IT IS WHEN KINDRED LIVE TOGETHER IN UNITY!"
—Psalm 133:1

. . . . .

of his Anglican friends. Finally, his celibate priesthood and identity as a serious poet further isolated him.

Like a good steward, Hopkins did not allow his bouts with suffering to go to waste. He prayed and worked his way through loneliness, molding from this gritty clay poems that speak to wounded hearts. Even in the depths of depression, Hopkins clung to Christ, refusing to give up on life: "Mine, O thou lord of life, send my roots rain."[1]

Although all of Hopkins' "terrible sonnets" convince solitary readers that he is on intimate terms with loneliness, I have found my greatest comfort in "To seem the stranger." Written in Dublin where he was teaching, this poem expresses the layers of Hopkins' loneliness. Yet it also acknowledges the "kind love" he is able to offer and receive from his fellow Jesuits.

How many of us who have separated from family and place of origin have not felt as the poet does in his opening stanza?

> To seem the stranger lies my lot, my life
> Among strangers. Father and mother
>   dear,
> Brothers and sisters are in Christ not near
> And he my peace my parting, sword and
>   strife.[2]

Hopkins is in a foreign land, not only geographically but also domestically. His conversion to Catholicism made him, in some sense, a stranger to his own family. Because he is not in his English homeland, he finds it even more difficult than usual to form the friendships that would ease his isolation. Christ himself is a source of both peace and strife in the poet's life.

However, despite these deprivations, Hopkins assures us that his "removes" do not shut him off completely from others: "...Not but in all removes I can / Kind love both give and get."[3] The dark veil of loneliness parts long enough

. . . . .

"POETRY IS A WAY OF TAKING LIFE BY THE THROAT."
—Robert Frost

. . . . .

"WHO WILL SEPARATE US FROM THE LOVE OF CHRIST?"
—Romans 8:35

. . . . .

for him to see that it is not the all-embracing reality it often seems.

Reading Gerard Manley Hopkins, his life and his work, we can be strengthened by his triumphs over suffering, his joy in nature as a constant solace, and his ability to say on his deathbed: "I am so happy. I am so happy."

The life of Jessica Powers (1905–1988), by contrast, was characterized by companionship with family, friends, fellow poets and, later, her Carmelite sisters. No doubt she experienced loneliness during her years as a single woman in Chicago and New York. Having been raised on a Wisconsin farm, Powers often yearned for the simplicity and landscapes of her childhood.

At the age of thirty-six the poet entered the cloister and began her inner exploration of the landscapes of solitude. Her work is inundated with awareness of the God who resides within. It reflects as well her deep understanding of the human condition, the "agony and the ecstasy" of our ordinary lives.

We find ourselves readily empathizing with Powers in "I Measure Loneliness." The opening stanza validates our own estimates of loneliness' reach:

> I measure loneliness,
> spreading the tape from chime to evening
>   chime,
> and it is taller than the sky's blue stress
> and lengthier than time.[4]

A day, even in a cloister where reminders of God's presence are everywhere, can seem to stretch for miles when we are shrouded in unbidden aloneness. The poet admits that she had not guessed how far "out into the unknown" loneliness can extend. We may be convinced, for a time, that it has no limits.

Yet in her final stanza, Powers begins to see clearly that "time's measures all are fraud and artifice." Only God knows the true measure of our loneliness. And when we have given

. . . . .

"TO A POET NOTHING CAN BE USELESS."
—Samuel Johnson

. . . . .

"THE NURSE OF FULL-GROWN SOULS IS SOLITUDE."
—James Russell Lowell

. . . . .

ourselves to him, we do not set boundaries with rulers, clocks or calendars. As the poet concludes: "No one on earth could mark the miles I go."[5]

In my own attempts to sort out loneliness from solitude, I find that line as reassuring as an answered prayer.

CONTEMPORARY WISDOM

Among the modern masters who sorted out solitude from loneliness was Anthony de Mello, S.J., author and retreat director. The first time I saw him in a video presentation, I was offended at the obvious satisfaction he took in jolting people out of their Catholic comfort zones. It took me awhile to recognize that my dismay was a symptom of my own reluctance to be elbowed out of those same zones.

Awareness was de Mello's constant theme. He loved nothing better than to awaken hidebound Christians, Muslims or Jews to the ways in which their beliefs often stunted their faith. As he summed it up: "Your beliefs give you a lot of security, but faith is insecurity."[6]

Living in insecurity meant, in de Mello's view, overcoming our resistance to change and opening our minds to understand, listen and challenge our unexamined beliefs. Those beliefs include our inherited or inculcated ideas about love, loneliness and happiness. The popular retreat director began by insisting that the desire for unconditional happiness is not selfish, and that we do not need other people to be happy. It is necessary for us to love, but not to be loved. (I balked at that lesson until Saint Francis of Assisi cleared his throat and recited, "O Divine Master grant that I may not so much seek to be loved as to love...")

In a chapter called "Addictive Love," DeMello points out that needing people leads us to use them for our own purposes. We habitually manipulate them to fulfill our needs and desires.

> When I die to the need for people, then
> I'm right in the desert. In the beginning it

. . . . .

"THE WAY OF SALVATION IS EASY; IT IS ENOUGH TO LOVE."

—Margaret of Cortona

. . . . .

feels awful, it feels lonely, but if you can take it for awhile, you'll suddenly discover that it isn't lonely at all. It is solitude, it is aloneness, and the desert begins to flower.[7]

The Jesuit mentor advises us that those who have the courage to endure loneliness will discover the comfort of solitude. Most of us, however, are seeking a quick fix, a connection, a way out of our own company. Any feeble distraction will do. We fear the desert and defy the cactus to bloom.

DeMello draws our attention to Jesus. Was he not alone in the desert and on the mountain? When he lost himself in prayer for those he had left behind, was he not engaging in an act of love? Jesus understood that to love "means to see a person, a situation, a thing as it really is, not as you imagine it to be. And to give it the response it deserves."[8]

Once we open ourselves to reality, we drop the illusion of needing to be loved. "Loneliness is not cured by human company," de Mello writes. "Loneliness is cured by contact with reality."[9] When we refuse to face the emptiness inside ourselves, we take refuge in unreality. But growth stops. The Eden of solitude remains barred.

> . . . . .
> "It is good when a soul loves solitude; it's a sign that it takes delight in God and enjoys speaking with him."
> —Jane Frances de Chantal
> . . . . .

Holy Laughter/Leisure

Solitude is a state we, as spiritual seekers, theoretically desire. Often enough, however, when the opportunity to experience it comes along, we suddenly have pressing business elsewhere. The rounded loveliness of the word itself rolls off our tongues like the name of a cherished loved one. Yet we back away from the prospect of being alone in our rooms for the interminable span of twenty minutes.

Only when we overcome our fear of solitude do we realize that we need never be lonely again. So, what it is we fear? I dread the train of thoughts that will come rattling into my brain like a runaway locomotive. One car will be brimming with worries I have sidestepped while at work. Another will be packed with self-judgments and feelings of inadequacy. Yet another will overflow with concerns about family, people in the news, and the "sorry state" of the church or the world at the time.

When I give in to this dread, I am abdicating any responsibility for allowing the train to pass through without examining its contents. I am pretending that someone outside myself is forcing me to react to these intrusions into solitude's tranquil domain.

What else do I fear? Shorn of distractions, I must confront the reality that I am alone. Feelings of unworthiness and separateness, stored in the subconscious, may come crawling under the doorjamb, demanding attention. It is safer to keep these gremlins locked below.

Finally, most difficult to confess, is the fear that the God who speaks in silence might draw me even further into solitude where I will no longer feel in control of this intimate relationship. I may be called further than I am prepared to go in love, compassion and peacemaking. I fear the changes that will be required by the One who says: "I am about to do a new thing; / now it springs forth, do you not perceive it?" (Isaiah 43:19).

Therefore, to my shame, I often avoid the holy leisure of solitary prayer. The Lord offers to cure my loneliness. But I demur, saying, "Maybe tomorrow, when I'm not so busy, so tired, so distracted, so leery of being alone with You."

The mentor who has most often persuaded me to venture out from the shore onto the shimmering green sea of solitude is Saint Teresa of Avila. Mystic she may be, but she is practical as a fishwife in her guidance on contemplative prayer. Because she herself managed to avoid contemplation for many years, we recognize our kinship with her and willingly listen to what she has to say.

"For mental prayer in my opinion," she observes, "is

. . . . .

"WE FEAR TO BE ALONE, AND TO BE OURSELVES, AND SO TO REMIND OTHERS OF THE TRUTH THAT IS IN THEM."
—Thomas Merton

. . . . .

nothing else than an intimate sharing between friends; it means taking time frequently to be alone with Him who we know loves us."[10]

In that simple statement, Teresa grounds us in two basic truths. The Lord to whom we pray has called us friends. Would it not be self-defeating and contradictory of us to avoid spending time with friends we love? The "with" is a reminder that our perceived "aloneness" is a fiction. "And remember, I am with you always, to the end of the age" (Matthew 32:20).

Whether we choose to be with Jesus in wordless silence or in quiet conversation does not matter. Teresa generously advises us to pray as we are able, rather than striving to become miscast mystics. She recommends beginning with the basics: Who am I? To Whom am I speaking when I pray? How can I most authentically communicate with the One to whom I pray?

When we are tempted to give up solitary prayer because it is "ruined" by distractions, Teresa demands, "Get used to it!" Like an elder sister encouraging her siblings, she reveals: "I know quite well that you are capable of it—for I endured this trial for many years of being unable to concentrate on one subject, and a very sore trial it is."[11]

Though we are convinced that we have not truly prayed and are no more inspired than if we had recited the alphabet, persistence in solitary prayer is the key. The Lord never leaves us stranded or denies us his friendship. There is no standardized test for acceptable prayer. "And if we cannot succeed in one year," Teresa says, "we will succeed later. Let's not regret the time that is so well spent. Who's making us hurry?"[12]

Our stock excuses for avoiding solitary prayer will never get us off Teresa's hook. She sees through them all into our self-protective hearts. Her confidence that persevering in prayer will lead us into the joys of solitude is irresistible. If we are humble enough and pay more attention to our

. . . . .

"WHAT MAKES
THE DESERT
BEAUTIFUL...
IS THAT
SOMEWHERE
IT HIDES A WELL."
—Antoine de
Saint-Exupery

. . . . .

"BLESSED ARE
THOSE WHO ARE
GLAD TO HAVE
TIME TO SPARE
FOR GOD."
—Thomas à
Kempis

. . . . .

Companion than to our poor performance, we will begin to anticipate our daily time alone.

Accepting Teresa's guidance, I have tried the following one-on-one ways of keeping company with Jesus—especially in times of loneliness.

- Praying a vocal prayer like the Our Father line by line while considering the meaning of each petition in my own life. The saint's advice is: "Pray the Our Father—but take an hour to pray it."[13]

- Praying with a favorite icon, like "The Storm on the Sea of Galilee" in which Peter and John beseech Jesus' intercession. Because he is calmly sleeping, they assume he has left them to face the storm alone. Their doubting of his awareness of them reminds me that Jesus may seem to be snoozing when we are alone together. I do not have to shake him awake to guarantee his attention. The saint's advice is: "You will find it very helpful if you can get an image…of this Lord—one that you like—to use regularly whenever you talk to Him"[14]

- Praying with as few words as possible while keeping mind and heart focused on my Partner in dialogue. I may not be able to sustain this prayer for more than ten minutes. But, in humility, I do not label these small attempts "failures." The saint's advice is: "Those who are able to shut themselves up in this way within this little Heaven of the soul, wherein dwells the Maker of Heaven and earth…may be sure that they are walking on an excellent road."[15]

- Praying faithfully the Liturgy of the Hours or selected psalms that match my mood when lonely, depressed, or convinced that my prayers are "dead letters sent / To dearest him that lives alas! away."[16] The saint's advice is: "When I find myself trammeled by weakness, lukewarmness, lack of mortification and many other things, I realize that I must beg for help from the Lord."[17]

All of these approaches, together with my most con-
genial way of praying through spiritual reading and writing,
have led me along the excellent road Teresa traveled. The
reality I've come to recognize is this: The further I move
into prayer, the harder it is for lonesomeness to touch me.
Conversely, the less I rely on prayer and seek the thicket of
distractions, the more readily I am snared. It is that simple.

REFLECT

How have you experienced the difference between loneliness and aloneness or solitude?

What are the positive steps you are willing to take to seek
comfort in your loneliness?

PRAY

O Divine Comforter,
encompass the lonely heart,
the soul dwindled by disconnection.
Comfort, comfort
all the alienated and alone.
Embrace our poverty.
Empower us to bloom in arid
places.
Amen.

. . . . .

"IN THE
MORNING, WHILE
IT WAS STILL VERY
DARK, HE GOT UP
AND WENT OUT
TO A DESERTED
PLACE, AND
THERE HE
PRAYED."
—Mark 1:35

. . . . .

NOTES

1. "Thou art indeed just," Gerard Manley Hopkins. *A Commentary on the Sonnets of G. M. Hopkins*, Peter Milward, S.J. (Chicago: Loyola University Press, 1969), p. 182.

2. "To seem the stranger," *Ibid.*, p. 152.

3. *Ibid.*

4. "I Measure Loneliness," *Selected Poetry of Jessica Powers*, Regina Siegfried and Robert Morneau, ed. (New York: Sheed & Ward, 1989), p. 114.

5. *Ibid.*

6. Anthony de Mello, *Awareness*, ed. J. Francis Stroud, S.J. (New York: Doubleday, 1990), p. 18.

7. *Ibid.*, p. 141.

8. *Ibid.*, p. 161.

9. *Ibid.*, p. 55.

10. *The Book of Her Life, The Collected Works of St. Teresa of Avila*, ed. Kieran Kavanaugh, O.C.D. and Otilio Rodriguez, O.C.D. (Washington, DC: ICS Publications, 1976), p. 96.

11. *The Way of Perfection*, St. Teresa of Avila, ed. E. Allison Peers (New York: Doubleday, 1964), pp. 173-74.

12. *Ibid.*

13. *Ibid.*, p. 125.

14. *Ibid.*, p. 177.

15. *Ibid.*, p. 185.

16. "I wake and feel," Milward, p. 158.

17. *The Way of Perfection*, p. 275.

Five

BE COMFORTED IN YOUR SICKNESS
A healing chapter for the ailing

"THIS IS MY COMFORT IN MY DISTRESS,
THAT YOUR PROMISE GIVES ME LIFE."
—PSALM 119:50

. . . . .

STORY TIME

It was good to be home again. No matter how accommodating they were, the appeal of European hotels always waned after a few days. The trip to France was an annual event, undertaken on behalf of the pharmaceutical company for which she worked. At the convention she had spent ten-hour days standing at the company booth. So when her left leg caused sudden pain, she thought immediately of those tedious days of remaining on her feet in constant discomfort.

Now she was having trouble breathing. Never a person to play around with illness, Marisa consulted her family doctor. He suspected that she might have a blood clot in her left leg and that it had been caused by the hours of inactivity on her transatlantic flight. She rarely paced the aisles on a plane, preferring not to draw attention to herself. Now she wished she had been more assertive about getting out of her cramped seat.

Although her physician scheduled tests for the following day, Marisa found herself in the hospital by evening. She was coughing up blood and could hardly breathe. Her pulse had slowed, her temperature dropped to 93. Marisa was rushed to the emergency room for treatment of an embolism that was blocking the flow of blood to her lungs.

While the medical team worked to keep her alive, the patient fought to keep breathing. At thirty-five she was horrified by the prospect of death. "I'm too young to die. I can't go now," she insisted to the chaplain who was anointing her. The oxygen mask, despite its beneficial purpose, unreasonably irritated her.

As a last-resort drug to break the blood clot was injected, Marisa remembered that she had not yet prayed. "How strange," she mused, as though speculating about a stranger's odd behavior. "God, help me," she said. "I'm so cold, so cold."

Later when she awoke in the intensive care unit, Marisa recognized the faces of her husband and her mother bending over her. She absorbed instant comfort from their presence. Words would have been an intrusion. Tom kissed her, holding her face lightly in both hands. She was certain that death would not be stopping for her that day.

Her mother stroked her hand exactly as she had when Marisa was five and heading for her first day at kindergarten. "Baby," she said, "you had a massive blood clot. But you're going to be all right, thank God."

The patient did not have the energy to speak. But as she returned her mother's intense gaze, God's love enveloped her as surely as the warm air "cocoon" the nurses had used to raise her body temperature. Marisa had survived. And she was exhausted.

Drifting back into sleep, the patient did not know that there were weeks of recuperation ahead of her. There would be diagnostic tests, medications, complications and setbacks. She had not seen the end of pain or fears about her body's reliability.

However, there would be no more doubts about staying alive. Marisa knew, with the certainty of Lazarus stumbling out of the tomb, trailing his winding sheets, that the Lord meant her to take hold of life. She whispered, "Thank you, God. Thank you."

Her final waking thought was, "Now I know why some wise person said that if our only prayer was 'Thank you,' that would be enough. It is."

. . . . .

"A WISE [PERSON]
SHOULD
CONSIDER THAT
HEALTH IS THE
GREATEST OF
HUMAN
BLESSINGS, AND
LEARN HOW BY
HIS OWN
THOUGHT TO
DERIVE BENEFIT
FROM HIS [HER]
ILLNESSES."
—Hippocrates

. . . . .

SCRIPTURAL VOICES

When illness topples me from my steed "Self-Reliant," I need to hear two voices from the Bible by my bedside. They originate in different provinces of the book, separated by centuries and generations. However, the harmony they create outlasts all generations. It soothes the ailing heart. It touches the aching body.

The voices belong to the prophet Isaiah of Israel and the rabbi Jesus of Nazareth. Their synchronicity is attested to by Jesus himself who moved from Nazareth to Capernaum in fulfillment of Isaiah's prophecy: "Galilee of the Gentiles, the people who sat in darkness have seen a great light" (Matthew 4:15–16). Jesus confirms it again when he reads from the scroll of Isaiah in the synagogue to identify himself as the one anointed by the Lord to bring glad tidings to the poor, the sick, and the oppressed. (See Luke 4:16–21 and Isaiah 61:1–3.)

To those who are sick in spirit, body or mind, these two physicians speak God's healing words. Reading these voices aloud, or asking someone to do it for you, may enable you to push back the walls of your sickroom, making space for empathetic others to join you. Invite them in—the sinner, the paralytic, the weak-kneed and feeble, the fevered, the blind and the deaf, the depressed and possessed—all to whom Jesus has said, "What do you want me to do for you?"

If you have trouble hearing them, open your Bible, find one of their stories, and identify with these seekers of healing. Allow the prophet and the rabbi to tend to your care.

. . . . .

"LOVE
COMFORTETH
LIKE SUNSHINE
AFTER RAIN."
—Shakespeare

. . . . .

Isaiah:

> Comfort, O comfort my people,
>   says your God.
> Speak tenderly to Jerusalem,
>   and cry to her
> that she has served her term,
>   that her penalty is paid,
> that she has received from the LORD's hand
>   double for all her sins. (40:1–2)

Jesus:

"Which is easier, to say to the paralytic, 'Your sins are forgiven,' or to say, 'Stand up and take your mat and walk'? But so that you may know that the Son of Man has authority on earth to forgive sins'—he said to the paralytic—'I say to you, stand up, take your mat and go to your home'" (Mark 2:9–11).

Isaiah:
> Strengthen the weak hands,
>> and make firm the feeble knees.
> Say to those who are of a fearful heart,
>> "Be strong, do not fear!
> Here is your God.
>> He will come with vengeance,
> With terrible recompense.
>> He will come and save you."
> Then the eyes of the blind shall be opened,
>> and the ears of the deaf unstopped;
> then the lame shall leap like a deer,
>> and the tongue of the speechless sing for joy. (35:3–6)

. . . . .
"LET NOTHING
DISTURB YOU...
PATIENCE GAINS
ALL THINGS."
—Teresa of Avila

. . . . .

Jesus: [to the two blind men]
"Do you believe that I am able to do this?" [Then he touched their eyes and said] "According to your faith let it be done to you" (Matthew 9:28–29).

Isaiah:
> He will feed his flock like a shepherd;
>> he will gather the lambs in his arms,
> and carry them in his bosom,
>> and gently lead the mother sheep. (40:11)

Jesus:
"Come to me, all you that are weary and are carrying heavy burdens, and I will give you rest. Take my yoke upon you, and learn from me; for I am gentle and humble in heart, and you will find rest for your souls. For my yoke is easy, and my burden is light" (Matthew 11:28–30).

Isaiah:
> He gives power to the faint,
>> and strengthens the powerless.

...[T]hose who wait for the LORD shall renew
>   their strength,
> they shall mount up with wings like eagles,
> they shall run and not be weary,
>   they shall walk and not faint. (40:29, 31)

Jesus:

"Who touched me?...Someone touched me; for I noticed that power had gone out from me." [To the woman with a hemorrhage who had spent all her money on doctors without finding comfort] "Daughter, your faith has made you well; go in peace" (Luke 8:45–46, 48).

Isaiah:

> "As a mother comforts her child,
>   so I will comfort you" (66:13).

Jesus:

"What do you want me to do for you?" (Luke 18:41).

SPIRITUAL KIN

The author of *The Book of Divine Comfort* would be pleased to find twenty-first–century Christians coming to him for guidance. Meister Eckhart was a medieval mystic, scholastic and preacher who enjoyed teaching the common folk in the pews. When accused by a jealous archbishop of misleading the laity who flocked to his sermons, Eckhart replied, "If ignorant people are not taught, they will never learn, nor will they know how to live or die."[1] (In the fourteenth century, the laity, unlike ourselves, were unlettered. Thus, they were especially grateful for a preacher who respected them enough to share his considerable wisdom with them.)

The "Meister" (master or teacher) took pleasure in guiding Christians through the processes of thinking, reflecting and meditating on their faith. He hoped to share with them his own passionate conviction of God's nearness to humanity.

. . . . .

"SUFFERING IS A
SHORT PAIN AND
A LONG JOY."
—Henry Suso

. . . . .

Those who are sick or afflicted in any way are his primary "students" in *The Book of Divine Comfort*. Although it was
written seven centuries ago, Eckhart's work continues to
offer solace to those who can hear his singular voice. The
final third of his book is addressed to sufferers of physical
pain or mental anguish.

Eckhart begins by pointing out that since the Son of
God became human and suffered, we are mistaken if we
think we should be exempted from suffering. He reminds us
that the just are tried as gold in a furnace before God takes
them to himself. (See Wisdom 3:1–6.)

> If people could only know and consider
> how great the joy that God [in his own
> way], the angels, and all who know and
> love God, have in human patience, by
> which a man bears pain, misery, and loss
> for God's sake, they would find in that
> knowledge sufficient reason to be com-
> forted. [2]

Insisting that God is with us when we suffer, Eckhart wonders what more comfort we would want. We pray "Thy will
be done," but when God's will involves pain or affliction of
any kind, we quickly register our complaints. God, however, suffers gladly with us and for us. And he suffers "without anguish" when we accept tribulation for his sake.

> Suffering is then bliss to him and gives
> him no agony. If, therefore, we were what
> we should be, we should find in suffering,
> not anguish, but blessing and comfort. [3]

With parental practicality, the Meister reminds us that if we
are appeased by the consolations of our family and friends,
how is it that we do not find even greater solace in God's
infinite compassion? Those who through prayer and meditation nurture their awareness of God's presence will know

that they are "wrapped in God's love."

The teacher then tells a story about a sick man who declined to pray for good health. Asked why, he gave three reasons: 1) God would not have allowed him to get sick unless it was "best for him"; 2) A good person asks for what God wants rather than what he or she wants; 3) A return to good health is "too small a thing" to request of so "rich, loving, and bountiful [a] God."[4]

The sick man compares asking for health to a traveler who endures a hundred-mile journey to see the Pope only to ask him for a bean. Just as we are about to object to this comparison, Eckhart gives us pause.

> Now this I say, and it is a sure matter, that compared to God all good things, even all creation, is less than a bean. Therefore, with good reason, if I am a good and wise man, I shall be ashamed if I pray to be made well again.[5]

While we are still sputtering, Eckhart goes on to contrast the manner in which a Christian bears illness with the sufferings endured by "hucksters." The peddler puts up with arduous journeys, inclement weather, hunger, lack of sleep and constant discomfort for the sake of an uncertain profit. The Christian, who hopes for an eternal reward, should therefore be willing to endure whatever suffering sickness entails out of love for God.

Whether we agree entirely with Meister Eckhart's approach or not, he has given us a healthful broth to either sip or swig heartily when we have been felled by illness.

. . . . .

"SOMETIMES A CALL TO SPIRITUAL SOLITUDE AND LIBERTY MAY COME TO US MASKED AS A HUMILIATING SICKNESS OR WEAKNESS."
—Thomas Merton

. . . . .

CREATIVE WORKS

Illness builds a bridge or a wall. We choose whether to connect more closely with the world around us or retreat into our sick room. However, as Robert Frost observed, "Before I built a wall I'd ask to know / What I was walling in or walling out."[6]

Some choose to wall out others because those others are insufficiently solicitous or seem to have no understanding of the patient's burden. Alternatively, the barrier may be raised by an afflicted person who "does not want to be a burden to anyone" or who thinks that "suffering in silence" is the path to canonization. Pride and scrupulosity are experienced masons.

When we are sick, bridge building or repairing might well be our chief occupation. Our need to give and receive love, to reach out and to be held cannot be ignored. Do we deny this human need, mislabeling it "weakness"? Dom Hubert van Zeller reveals the truth of the matter to us:

> We always imagine that if we felt strong,
> we would not mind having to carry the
> Cross. But the whole point is that we
> should not feel strong. It is our weakness
> that very often is our chief cross.[7]

In our weakness, who or what crosses the bridge to bring us comfort? Beyond the family and friends who are Christ in the flesh for us, there are multiple sources from creation and creative works that may ease our pain, soothe our worried brow.

Anyone who is well enough to allow Mother Nature to tend him or her can: Lie in a hammock or on a porch swing and be braced by birdsong; sit in a garden and absorb the serenity on the faces of flowers; hug an oak tree and assimilate its strength; keep vigil by an unshaded window and attain a wider perspective on the stars; watch a thunderstorm and be charged with nature's unharnessed power.

In times of illness when unable to relate to nature directly, I have been cheered by scenic videos. A friend gave me one that I return to as ritually as to vitamin C for nagging colds. "The Wonder of Creation: Ireland" weds the pastoral beauty of landscapes to sacred music like "Morning

. . . . .

"WITHOUT THE BURDEN OF AFFLICTIONS IT IS IMPOSSIBLE TO REACH THE HEIGHT OF GRACE."
—Rose of Lima

. . . . .

"MAKE SICKNESS ITSELF A PRAYER."
—Francis de Sales

. . . . .

Has Broken" and "Jesus Loves Even Me."

Even when I was debilitated by strep throat, this collection of illustrated songs propped me up on sensory pillows. My scant bedroom opened out onto the green fields of Ireland, the commanding Cliffs of Moher, the barren beauty of the burrens, the seaside cliffs where sheep and cattle graze. The gentle pace of Irish life, symbolized by the farmer leading his dairy herd down the main road, reminded me that sickness imposes a contemplative lifestyle, whether we choose it or not.

Watching a mild rain filling rock bowls, I hummed the accompanying "Be Thou My Vision" and was comforted by the melancholy voice of a cello. I soared with the tin whistle on "Morning Has Broken," enjoying my kinship with the graceful deer browsing in the forest. Their gaze held mine in a moment of communion.

When the camera focused on a blue and white fishing boat anchored in the bay, I sensed its readiness to pursue the business of the day. Then, before I could register my own incapability of pursuing the daily round, the focus moved to a gray rowboat half-beached on the shore. The scene assured me that there is a time for sailing out to trade, and a time for resting on the sand. And the choice is made for us by another.

The nursing Nature offers can be paired with poetry to double our consolation. W.B. Yeats's "The Lake Isle of Innisfree" rocks us in the maternal arms of its soft rhythm, its repeated, lapping "l" sounds. The poem carries us off in our pajamas to "live alone in the bee-loud glade."[8]

Emily Dickinson's "The Mystery of Pain," on the other hand, recognizes our occasional conviction that pain seems to have no limits. We cannot remember its beginning nor can we imagine there was "a day when it was not." The poet comforts us by sharing the reality of her own affliction over which her creativity triumphed.[9]

. . . . .

"SUFFERING CHANGES AN EARTHLY PERSON INTO A HEAVENLY PERSON."
—Henry Suso

. . . . .

"TO TREAT LIFE AS LESS THAN A MIRACLE IS TO GIVE UP ON IT."
—Wendell Berry

. . . . .

With his "A Psalm of Life," Henry Wadsworth Longfellow encourages us to anticipate the day when we "shall take heart again." Life is far more than suffering, greater than sorrow. The poet will not allow us to sink back into bed, giving up on what lies ahead:

> Life is real—life is earnest—
> And the grave is not its goal:
> Dust thou art, to dust returnest,
> Was not spoken of the soul. [10]

Finally, we come full circle to Mary Oliver's "When Death Comes." A consummate poet of creation, Oliver breaks our hearts with her acute appreciation of nature's complexity. She sees all living creatures, from the common field daisy to the sad swans on the River Ayr, as "a brotherhood and sisterhood."

While she is alive, Oliver insists on immersing herself in earth's bounty. She refuses to stand apart, a tourist taking pictures with her fleeting glance:

> When it is over, I want to say: all my life
> I was a bride married to amazement.
> I was the bridegroom, taking the world
> into my arms. [11]

Mary Oliver's intense involvement in life shames us into embracing our own under-appreciated lives, even in sickness or other affliction. We surpass our narrow selves, and before we know it, are trying on bridal veils or dinner jackets. Recognizing why Robert Frost said "Poetry is a way of taking life by the throat," we rouse ourselves to get on with it.

. . . . .

"SPRING IS CHRIST, RAISING MARTYRED PLANTS FROM THEIR SHROUDS."
—Rumi

. . . . .

"SUFFERING OUT OF LOVE FOR GOD IS BETTER THAN WORKING MIRACLES."
—John of the Cross

. . . . .

CONTEMPORARY WISDOM

On March 30, 1990, a shooting star went home to heaven. Her name was Sister Thea Bowman and she was an African American Franciscan Sister of Perpetual Adoration. She died of bone cancer after long suffering. But she did not leave the church she loved without first passing on her wisdom about how to live with serious illness.

Thea Bowman never walked into a room without drawing all eyes to herself. Her physical presence was large, vibrant, beautiful and bold. As an evangelist and gospel singer, she used her dramatic voice to lift people on wings of faith. Her persuasive powers were such that she once at a conference convinced the American bishops to hold hands and sing "We Shall Overcome."

Asked by a reporter how she felt about Catholic women not being allowed to preach in church, Thea Bowman replied that she would preach on the street corners or wherever she could get anyone to listen. She lived her faith fully, drawing people of all races together in a church where she had been wounded by racial prejudice.

When she was diagnosed with cancer, Sister Thea resolved to make each day count. She had "always asked God for the grace to live until [she] died." That grace was given and fully invested.

In an interview with Patrice J. Tuohy in *U.S. Catholic* (June 1990), Sister Thea shared her insights on suffering. She admitted that she could make no sense out of pain and affliction. However, she tried each day to remain open to people, laughter and love. Her frequent prayers were "Oh Jesus, I surrender" and "Father, take this cross away. Not my will, but thy will be done."

As a musician, Thea found great consolation in the spiritual songs on which she had been raised. Her responses to the interviewer's questions are interwoven with time-polished lyrics on living with tribulation. She relied on lyrics like "Sooner will be done the troubles of this world" and "Hold on just a little while longer. Everything is going to be all right."

Asked what good could come from suffering like hers, the Franciscan observed that it might be "an incentive" for

. . . . .

"LIFE WASTES ITSELF WHILE WE ARE PREPARING TO LIVE."
—Ralph Waldo Emerson

. . . . .

"GOD WHISPERS TO US IN OUR PLEASURES, SPEAKS TO US IN OUR CONSCIENCE, BUT SHOUTS TO US IN OUR PAINS."
—C.S. Lewis

. . . . .

human beings to help and love one another, "to be blessed and strengthened and humanized in the process." Suffering had helped her to clarify her relationships with God and with others. It had given her perspective on life and reminded her of her own inestimable value as a daughter of God.

Thea Bowman revealed that her faith had been simplified by her illness. "When I'm in pain," she said, "I know I need Jesus to walk with me. I can't make it on my own. I pray, 'Lord, I believe. Increase my faith. Help my unbelief.'" Her images of God remained those of her family: God as mother to the motherless, comforter, burden-bearer, heart-fixer, "my doctor who never lost a patient."

After six years of being assaulted by cancer, Thea was at times tempted to pray for an immediate healing or death. However, she resisted issuing that ultimatum and went on serving the Lord in whatever ways remained open to her. When she could no longer travel, even with her wheelchair, she ministered by smiling at, listening to, and encouraging others.

Thea discovered that her own neediness and obvious depletion opened others' hearts more readily to her. People were more willing to tell her that they loved her, more ready to hear that they were loved in return. She helped them to understand how important it is for those who visit the sick to be at peace with themselves so they can radiate peace to the patient.

Asked what words of encouragement she could share with her brothers and sisters in suffering, Thea Bowman generously responded:

> To the suffering I say, "Try to reach out to others. Try to let people know how much you love them. Try to maintain a sense of humor and laughter in life. Try to keep in touch with the children and the elderly. Talk about what you're thinking and what

. . . . .

"MIRACLE OF MIRACLES THAT SO GREAT A GOD LIVES IN SO FRAIL A DWELLING."
—The Great Maggid

. . . . .

you're feeling. Talk about what you need and what you want. Talk about what you see, and talk about your experiences. Invite people to share a prayer with you. Generally, let people know where you are. Often folks will stand around waiting and wanting to help. Only you, as the sick person, can tell them what they can do."[12]

At her three-hour funeral in Jackson, Mississippi, Sister Thea was celebrated with song, laughter and tears. Her good friend, Father John Ford, spoke the words that she had given him: "Just say what Sojourner Truth said about her own eventual dying. Tell them what Sojourner Truth said: 'I'm not going to die. I'm going home like a shooting star.'"[13]

As Sister Thea Bowman's body was carried out of the church, the impassioned congregation sang, "I'll Fly Away."

HOLY LAUGHTER

After surgery ten years ago for malignant melanoma, I needed something to balance the scales which were decidedly tipping in favor of "Worries About Recurrence." My monthly visits to my friendly neighborhood oncologist were reassuring. But the simple fact that I had to check in every thirty days kept my low-grade stress percolating like overdone camp coffee.

I found comfort in two mismatched sources: *The New Yorker* cartoons and the Gospel of John. Both gave me cause for laughter, lowered my blood pressure and provided sunshine on cloudy days.

Although the Fourth Gospel is not generally cited as the most humorous book in the New Testament, it does contain the story of "The Man Born Blind Receives His Sight" (9:1–41). Anyone can read that story with an open mind and not break out in at least a foolish grin must be considered incurably grave.

. . . . .

"IT IS NOT GOD'S WILL THAT WE SHOULD LINGER OVER PAIN, BUT THAT WE SHOULD PASS QUICKLY THROUGH IT TO JOY WITHOUT END."

—Julian of Norwich

. . . . .

I cannot prove the following assertion. But I strongly suspect that a large percentage of subscribers to *The New Yorker* thumb directly past all the analytical and cultural articles to get at the cartoons. We may return to the articles after slurping up every last drop of humor poured out like a chocolate thickshake in every edition. And no one does medical cartoons better than this worthy magazine's contributors.

Whether I was in post-surgical pain or bent by worry, my condition was improved by periodic exposure to the comical drawings of Roz Chast, Leo Cullum, Frank Cotham and others. I could not help identifying with the man who receives the following prognosis from his physician: "It appears that you'll definitely outlive your usefulness" (Cullum).

Nor could I resist the cartoon "Get Well Immediately" card with its saucy verse: "Hope you'll soon be convalescing. / Please get well—you're so depressing" (Chast).

And it was impossible to take myself quite so seriously after seeing a doctor pull a sheet up over a dead patient's head while remarking to a colleague, "Shows how much I know" (Cotham).

However, the medicinal effect of these laugh-inducers pales by comparison with the story from John's Gospel. It is recorded with a completely straight face. But it would be shocking to discover that Jesus did not have a few good laughs at the antics of the blind man's parents and the Pharisees who purported not to be blind.

As the story begins, we see Jesus restoring the blind man's sight by spitting on the ground, making a mudpack, and spreading it on the man's eyes. These earthy details, appearing nowhere else in the Gospels, rivet our attention. Images of mother's mustard plasters slapped on our chests as children arise, piquing our interest in Jesus' robust bedside manner. John 9 will not be told in the usual just-the-facts style of the healing stories.

. . . . .

WE WORRY AWAY OUR LIVES, FEARING THE FUTURE, DISCONTENT WITH THE PRESENT, UNABLE TO TAKE IN THE IDEA OF DYING, UNABLE TO SIT STILL."
—Lewis Thomas

. . . . .

"I TOLD YOU I WAS SICK."
—a hypochondriac's epitaph

. . . . .

We are given a whiff of the humor to come when the man's neighbors are asked to identify him as the former blind beggar. They reply, "No, but it is someone like him" (9:9). With the exception of his eyes, he looks exactly as he did before. But, hedging their bets, they insist that he is merely a look-alike who happens to be at the pool of Siloa, where the blind beggar habitually stationed himself. This handy ruse will disqualify them as witnesses should they be called on by the authorities.

Then the "Case of the Mistaken Identity" is turned over to the Pharisees. They at first ignore the miracle's source while griping about its taking place on the Sabbath. They then refuse to accept the blind man's word for who he is, and insist on interviewing his parents. After all, they must know better who he is than he himself does.

The parents, however, like the neighbors, refuse to be put on the spot. Aware that the Pharisees want to disprove the miracle, they pass the buck by saying, "Ask him; he is of age. He will speak for himself" (9:21). Their fears for themselves, apparently, do not extend to their son. Let him take the rap. He's over eighteen.

Having struck out with the parents, the Pharisees return to cross-examining the son. How did a man who is a sinner manage to cure his blindness? The witness responds stubbornly: "I do not know whether he is a sinner. One thing I do know, that though I was blind, now I see" (9:25). (At this point, I can imagine a gospel choir lustily singing "Amazing Grace.") The man will not be swayed from the truth to save his hide. Hallelujah!

Like corrupt detectives, the Pharisees insist that he repeat his story for the third time. To which he replies: "Why do you want to hear it again? Do you also want to become his disciples?" (9:27). If he had had an inflatable vaudevillian billy club, the once-blind man could have bopped their heads while delivering that punch line.

. . . . .

"JESUS TREATS US WITH HUMOR, BECAUSE HE SURPASSES US, BECAUSE HE UNDERSTANDS US, BECAUSE HE TAKES OUR MEASURE AND LOVES US."
—Father Henri Cormier, C.J.M.

. . . . .

Huffily identifying themselves as disciples of Moses, the Pharisees claim they have no idea where Jesus comes from. The witness can hardly believe his ears. "Here is an astonishing thing!" he says, "You do not know where he comes from, and yet he opened my eyes" (9:30).

He goes on to instruct these experts that God listens only to those who worship him and do his will. If Jesus were a sinner, as they contend, he could not possibly heal a man blind from birth. Therefore, he is obviously from God.

Throwing out their chests like prize roosters, the Pharisees retort, "You were born entirely in sins, and you are trying to teach us?" (9:34). Before he can verbally best them again, they drive him out of the temple.

. . . . .

"NONE SO BLIND
AS THOSE THAT
WILL NOT SEE."
—Matthew
Henry

. . . . .

Justice wins the day as the man becomes Jesus' disciple, the Pharisees claim they are not blind, and Jesus finishes them off with "If you were blind, you would not have sin. But now that you say, 'We see,' your sin remains" (9:41). Then, if my guess is right, the Healer and his new recruit go off to share a decent meal and a jar of good Judean wine.

I have never been able to read or listen to this story without laughing at the hypocrisy of the Pharisees, the sly self-protection of the parents, and the chutzpah of the once-blind man. It is a tried-and-true home remedy for the blahs that accompany our lesser ailments.

We sometimes forget, especially during times of illness, that Jesus told his friends at the Last Supper: "I have said these things to you so that my joy may be in you, and that your joy may be complete" (John 15:11). His joy does not abandon us at the first sign of a cough or a fever.

As Cal Samra suggests in his book *The Joyful Christ: The Healing Power of Humor*, we need a National Association for Spiritual Health. And the chief physician would be the rabbi who said, "Those who are well have no need of a physician, but those who are sick" (Matthew 9:12).

REFLECT

In what ways has sickness ever been a blessing for you?
Who or what enables you to experience suffering as a blessing rather than a curse?

If someone suffering chronic illness or pain sought your
advice about how to cope with it, what might you say?
Why?

PRAY

O Divine Comforter,
tend the ailing heart,
the soul cramped by suffering.
Comfort, comfort
all the sick and infirm.
Lift us from pallets of self-pity.
Clothe us with your compassion.
Amen.

. . . . .

"THE MOST
WASTED DAY OF
ALL IS THAT ON
WHICH
WE HAVE NOT
LAUGHED."
—Sebastien
Chamfort

. . . . .

NOTES

1. Meister Eckhart, *The Book of Divine Comfort*, Raymond B. Blakney, trans. (New York: Harper & Row, 1941), p. 73.

2. *Ibid.*, pp. 65-66.

3. *Ibid.*, p. 67.

4. *Ibid.*, p. 71.

5. *Ibid.*

6. "Mending Wall," *The Poetry of Robert Frost*, Edward Connery Lathem, ed. (New York: Holt, Rhinehart & Winston, 1969), p. 34.

7. "Words for Quiet Moments," *Catholic Digest*, January 2003, p. 126.

8. "The Lake Isle of Innisfree," *Selected Poems*, W. B. Yeats (New York: Gramercy Books, 1992), p. 57.

9. "The Mystery of Pain," *Collected Poems of Emily Dickinson*, ed. Mabel Loomis Todd and J. W. Higginson (New York: Gramercy Books, 1982), p. 10.

10. "A Psalm of Life," Henry Wadsworth Longfellow, *America's Favorite Poems*, ed. Robert Pinsky and Maggie Dietz (New York: W. W. Norton, 2000), pp. 168-69.

11. "When Death Comes," *New and Selected Poems*, Mary Oliver (Boston: Beacon Press, 1992), p. 10.

12. "On the road to glory," Patrice J. Tuohy. *U. S. Catholic*, June 1990, pp. 27-30.

13. "'Shooting star' Bowman's gone home," Tom Fox. *National Catholic Reporter*, Apr. 13, 1990, p. 4.

Six

BE COMFORTED IN YOUR DYING
A healing chapter for those facing death

> PRECIOUS IN THE SIGHT OF THE LORD,
> IS THE DEATH OF HIS FAITHFUL ONES.
> —PSALM 116:15

STORY TIME

It was a place where people go to die. But its appearance was that of a sunlit lodge for sedate vacationers. The sign over the door read "St. Veronica's Hospice." Here the terminally ill were not turned away from or lied to about their imminent deaths. Veronica's was an oasis of truth in a death-denying culture.

The day Tom took his Uncle Louie to the hospice his relief at no longer being responsible for the patient's care overcame his guilt at passing on the burden. "It's their job," he assured himself. "They can do it a lot better than I can."

Louie's cancer was inoperable. He had no immediate family to care for him at home. Tom and his family had taken him in. But now that his uncle could no longer take morphine orally, Tom felt incapable of and unwilling to carry on. The opening at the hospice was a godsend.

There were no complaints from Louie over his transfer from his nephew's home. His suffering did not blind him to the effect he was having on Tom's family. Liz and the girls were visibly depressed by the sight of his emaciated body, his pain-lined face. He was also dimly aware that he had shouted at them when they did not immediately appear with his medications. He recalled shoving Liz aside like an intruder when she tried to soothe him. At night Tom and Liz had to alternate as nurses responding to his calls for water, morphine or turning him over in bed. It had crossed his mind that he must be ruining their sex life. But, in his misery, he thought, "Who are they to complain? When I'm gone, they'll have plenty of time for fooling around."

"So this is what dying is," he thought idly as the hospice nurses made sure he was comfortable. "I'll be glad when it's over." Then he fell into the reprieve of sleep, a little death from which he would surely rise.

Tom sat by the bed. He had planned to leave as soon as Uncle Louie was settled. Now he watched his dying uncle's labored breathing. The robust physique of the former baseball player had fallen in on itself like an aging barn. The cocksure voice of the athlete could no longer charm. Louie was passing.

Placing his hand on Louie's coverlet, Tom touched his uncle's skeletal arm with a few fingers, careful not to place any weight on so frail a resting place. He knew that the staff at St. Veronica's was dedicated to offering each patient an opportunity to experience "a good death." It seemed an oxymoron. But Tom knew that Louie's suffering would be alleviated as much as possible with painkillers and solicitous attention.

Everyone at the hospice entered a community that affirmed life and respected death as a necessary transition. Patients were listened to as intently as to accomplished homilists. If they needed to be reconciled with someone, that person would be invited to come in and make peace with the one whose time was short. It occurred to Tom that Louie might, after awhile, want to apologize to Liz and their daughters for his aggressive surliness.

Glancing at his watch, the visitor itched to leave. He could still beat the 5 P.M. traffic. However, he did not move. Uncle Louie held him without laying a hand on him or raising his voice. Now that he was no longer carrying his uncle over his shoulder, Tom had the energy to love him as he had as a child.

"Do you know how excited I used to be when you came to visit?" he silently inquired. "How thrilled I was to play catch with you and tell all my friends what a pro you were? You were, hands down, my favorite uncle. I still have the

. . . . .

"WE AWAIT THE FINAL OUTCOME OF EVENTS, REMEMBERING WHO IT IS WHO PLOWS THE EARTH OF OUR SOULS."
—Tertullian

. . . . .

"WE ARE ALL RESIGNED TO DEATH; IT'S LIFE WE AREN'T RESIGNED TO."
—Graham Greene

. . . . .

catcher's mitt you gave me for my seventh birthday. I was always glad you didn't give me dull books or Dr. Denton pajamas."

Tom gave free rein to the monologue of remembrance. Taking his watch off, he put it in his pocket. He would not leave until Louie woke up. The visitor was no longer so harried that he forgot that every "goodbye" now had momentous potential.

"You still here?" Louie asked, squinting at him. He loved the young man before him, the son he had never had. There were stories he wanted to share with Tom, a few things his own father had taught him. When he saw that his nephew held a black rosary in his right hand, he smiled. "Maybe you ought to get me one of those things," he said, nodding toward the beads. "I'm kind of out of practice, but I guess it's not too late yet."

When the aide brought his light supper, Louie reached for Tom's hand. "I'll be fine here. Don't worry," he said. Tom's throat tightened. He shook his uncle's hand, cradling the brittle fingers. "I know, Unc," he said. "See you tomorrow after work."

Louie looked down at his tray. "Thanks, son," he replied, and did not wipe his eyes until Tom was out of sight.

Scriptural Voices

When my mother died eight years ago, we prayed excerpts from the Liturgy of the Hours for her on the evening before her funeral. The extended family included several who no longer went to church. With their comfort in mind, we selected short sections of the New Testament readings, psalms and prayers from the Office of the Dead.

Mom was a seamstress who made patchwork quilts from remnants she found at fabric shops or yard sales. As I pieced together the following prayer, I borrowed her quilt-making process, substituting word-blocks for patches and assembling them in an original pattern.

. . . . .

"Think often of death, so as to prepare for it and appraise things at their true value."
—Charles de Foucauld

. . . . .

"I have seen so many people make a spiritual journey of their own that enables them to lay down their lives with peace."
—Dame Cicely Saunders

. . . . .

Had I suggested that analogy to her, she would have tucked her chin in just slightly, given me her diffident girl's smile, and searched my face to see if I was joking. It was her lifetime habit to devalue her own talents, focusing on the imperfect stitches or mismatched colors rather than the endearing beauty of each one-of-a-kind quilt, blessed by her hardworking hands.

Here, in abbreviated form, is the prayer quilt I put together for Mom. Those who are dying, together with those who keep vigil, might choose their own best-loved excerpts from the same source.

In the name of the Father...

"From the earth you formed me, with flesh you clothed me; Lord, my Redeemer, raise me up again at the last day."[1]

The voice of the psalmist is raised:

> I waited patiently for the LORD;
>> he inclined to me and heard my cry.
> He drew me up from the desolate pit,
>> out of the miry bog,
> and set my feet upon a rock,
>> making my steps secure...
>
> Be pleased, O LORD, to deliver me...
>> O LORD, make haste to help me...
>
> ...
> You are my help and my deliverer;
>> do not delay, O my God.
> (Psalm 40:1–2, 13, 17b)

Glory be to the Father...

The voice of Saint Paul assures us:

> Now if Christ is proclaimed as raised from
> the dead, how can some of you say there is
> no resurrection of the dead? If there is no

resurrection of the dead, then Christ has
not been raised; and if Christ has not been
raised, then our proclamation has been in
vain and your faith has been in vain....For
if the dead are not raised, then Christ has
not been raised....If for this life only we
have hoped in Christ, we are of all people
most to be pitied. But in fact Christ has
been raised from the dead, the first fruits
of those who have died. (1 Corinthians
15:12–14,16, 19–20)

Silent reflection on Christ's resurrection and our own

The voice of Paul continues:

> Listen, I will tell you a mystery! We will not
> all die, but we will all be changed, in a
> moment, in the twinkling of an eye, at the
> last trumpet. For the trumpet will sound,
> and the dead will be raised imperishable,
> and we will be changed. . .When this per-
> ishable body puts on imperishability, and
> this mortal body puts on immortality, then
> the saying that is written will be fulfilled:
> "Death has been swallowed up in victory."
> "Where, O death, is your victory?
> Where, O death, is your sting?"
> (1 Corinthians 15:51–52, 54–55)

. . . . .

"IN MY FATHER'S
HOUSE THERE ARE
MANY DWELLING
PLACES...
I GO TO PREPARE
A PLACE FOR
YOU."
—John 14:2

. . . . .

Silent reflection on Christ's victory over death, and ours.

The voice of Saint Paul concludes:

> So we do not lose heart. Even though our
> outer nature is wasting away, our inner
> nature is being renewed day by day. For
> this slight momentary affliction is prepar-
> ing us for an eternal weight of glory

> beyond all measure....For we know that
> if the earthly tent we live in is destroyed,
> we have a building from God, a house not
> made with hands, eternal in the heavens.
> ...So we are always confident; even
> though we know that while we are at
> home in the body we are away from the
> Lord—for we walk by faith, not by
> sight... (2 Corinthians 4:16–17, 5:1, 6–7)

Silent reflection on the source of our hope and confidence

Closing message of consolation:

> But we do not want you to be unin-
> formed, brothers and sisters, about those
> who have died, so that you may not
> grieve as others do who have no hope.
> For since we believe that Jesus died and
> rose again, even so, through Jesus, God
> will bring with him those who have died.
> (1 Thessalonians 4:13–14)

Our Father...

In the name of the Father...

. . . . .

"IF WE HAVE
KNOWN HOW TO
LIVE STEADFASTLY
AND CALMLY,
WE SHALL KNOW
HOW TO DIE IN
THE SAME WAY."
—Michel de
Montaigne

. . . . .

SPIRITUAL KIN

If we were to enroll in a how-to course on dying, we might choose as our professor Saint Thomas More. This sixteenth-century English statesman and writer has much to teach about the art of dying as believing Christians. To neglect his counsel is to be storm-tossed sailors ignoring a salutary lighthouse.

Sir Thomas More held the highest public office in England any commoner could attain: Lord High Chancellor. He and his second wife Alice, with their respective children and wards, enjoyed a comfortable estate in

Chelsea. There they frequently entertained More's wide circle of friends, including King Henry VIII.

While serving at Henry's pleasure, Thomas More was required to take an oath with which he did not agree. The oath essentially claimed that the king's marriage to Catherine of Aragon had not been a true marriage and that his subsequent marriage to Anne Boleyn had produced true successors to the throne. Since the pope had already affirmed that Henry's first marriage was valid, this oath denied the authority of the pope. More could not, in conscience, sign it.

Locked up in the Tower of London on April 13, 1534, Thomas More spent his time in prayer, writing letters of good counsel, and working on a book called *A Dialogue of Comfort*. Throughout his months in prison, More had to resist the entreaties of family and friends to take the oath and save himself. He employed his considerable wit to assure them that he could not "exchange eternity for twenty years." More begged his daughter Margaret not to use her brilliance to turn him aside from his conscience but to "be merry in God" that her father was remaining steadfast.

More composed his *Dialogue of Comfort* for all who fear pain and death. The dialogue is between two fictional characters, Uncle Anthony and his nephew Vincent. Anthony speaks in More's own voice about the necessity of meditating on the vanity of worldly things, on our own death, and on Christ's Passion.

These meditations, which More practiced faithfully in his prison cell, fortified his love for God and enabled him to not begrudge his fate. As Uncle Anthony advises Vincent: "...and take your cross of pain and passion upon your back, and die for the truth with [Christ], and thereby reign with him crowned in eternal glory."[2]

Whenever those who are suffering and dying feel too weak to endure, Anthony advises them to call on "our

. . . . .

"ON EARTH WE
ARE BUT
PILGRIMS."
—Teresa of Avila

. . . . .

captain Christ" and employ his strength against the tempta-tion to despair. More regrets the times in which he has shrunk from death and not considered "that in the saving of my body should stand the loss of my soul." With the help of the Holy Spirit, he embraces the truth that a person may "leese [lose] his head and yet have none harm, but instead of harm inestimable good at the hand of God."[3]

As he prays and writes, the prisoner grows hardier in spirit while his body deteriorates in the dank cell. He does not pray to be delivered from death "but referring all thing whole [entirely] unto his only pleasure, as to him that seeth better what is best for me than myself doth."[4]

Shortly before his arrest, Thomas More had composed a prayer which he wrote in the margins of his *Book of Hours*. This prayerbook accompanied him to the Tower. He seeks God's grace to ever be able to put first things first and to be content with whatever life hands him.

Among the prayer's petitions are these:

> To lean unto the comfort of God,
> Busily to labor to love him…
> To walk the narrow way that leadeth to life,
> To bear the cross with Christ;
> To have the last thing in remembrance,
> To have ever afore mine eye my death
> that is ever at hand…[5]

Saint Thomas More went to his death on the scaffold with consummate courage and wit. On the rickety stairs he joked, "I pray, Master Lieutenant, see me safe up, and for my coming down let me shift for myself." Kneeling, the con-demned man prayed Psalm 51 ("Have mercy on me, O God, / according to your steadfast love").

He then embraced his executioner and rallied him lest he fear to do his job. Referring to his own short neck, More advised, "Take heed thou strike not awry." He asked the crowd to pray for him and promised to return the favor. He requested that they pray for the king, and affirmed that he

. . . . .

"IN TWO
MOMENTOUS
MONOSYLLABLES,
DYING IS A
CHRISTIAN'S
FINAL 'I DO.' "
—Walter J.
Burghardt, S.J.

. . . . .

"died the king's good servant, but God's first." The advice he had given others about achieving a good death, Thomas More fulfilled in his own passing.

The book of More's life reveals the wisdom of not clinging to worldly goods or even to the loved ones who cannot accompany us on our final journey. It illustrates how prayer and meditation on the Passion of Christ can help us to overcome our last and greatest fear. It urges us to recognize that, with "our captain Christ" at our side, we can welcome Sister Death at our appointed hour.

CREATIVE WORKS

As director Ingmar Bergman has observed, a good film has the power to penetrate into "the twilight room of the soul." That insight is particularly apt when applied to the theme of death and dying. For those who have reached the final stage of their lives, there is comfort to be gained from reflecting on how certain film characters meet their deaths.

Among the films I have used on retreats, participants found the following inspiring in times of grave illness (their own or their loved ones'): *Shadowlands* (the story of how C.S. Lewis and his wife Joy prepare themselves for her death); *Jesus of Montreal* (in which an actor "becomes" the Christ he portrays in a Passion play); *The Mission* (depicting the opposite ways in which two Jesuit priests decide to confront certain death); and *Diary of a Country Priest* (the story of a devoted young priest who ministers to others as he himself is in the process of dying). In each of these films, characters meet death with compassionate concern for others and with minimal attention to their own redemptive suffering.

Although the lead character in *The Straight Story* does not die in the course of the film, the prospect of his brother's death and his own drives the narrative. The movie gained in poignancy for me when I learned that both the real-life Alvin Straight and the actor who portrayed him, Richard Farnsworth, died within two years of the film's completion.

. . . . .

"I'M ON THE LAST GREAT JOURNEY HERE—AND PEOPLE WANT ME TO TELL THEM WHAT TO PACK."
—Morrie Schwartz

. . . . .

Based on an actual pilgrimage made by seventy-three-year-old Alvin Straight to his brother Lyle's home over three hundred miles away, *The Straight Story* is a gentle meditation on preparing for death. Lyle Straight has suffered a stroke. His brother, from whom he has been estranged for ten years, is compelled to reconcile with him before it is too late.

At our first sight of Alvin, he is lying on the kitchen floor. He has fallen and is unable to get up. We soon learn that he has arthritic hips, emphysema, diabetes, circulation problems and fading eyesight. His doctor warns him that if he does not make some changes soon, there will be serious consequences.

Because he cannot qualify for a driver's license, Alvin decides to travel from Laurens, Iowa, to Mount Zion, Wisconsin, on his riding mower. He constructs a wooden trailer in which to sleep and store his supplies of coffee, wieners and lunchmeat.

Crawling along the open highway at a penitential pace, Alvin has time to reflect on the reason for his journey. The specific cause of his conflict with Lyle no longer matters. However, pride and vanity "mixed with liquor" motivated the squabble. "This trip," he later admits, "is a hard swallow to my pride." Yet he makes no complaints on his arduous travels through pastoral landscapes and across the Mississippi River.

Like a character out of Chaucer's *Canterbury Tales*, Alvin meets assorted fellow pilgrims along the way. He shares his wisdom and stories about what matters in life. With a young, runaway, single mother, he employs a symbol he has used with his own seven children. He contrasts the weakness of a single stick with a bundle of sticks that cannot be broken. The bundle is the family to whom she now chooses to return.

When he camps with a group of young, Lycra-clad cyclists, Alvin encourages them to enjoy their youth while realizing that it is ephemeral. He advises, "Learn to separate the wheat from the chaff and let the small stuff fall away."

At a bar with a fellow World War II veteran, the pilgrim shares his memories of being a sniper and of having mistakenly shot a scout from his own company. He recalls the "moon-faced boys" he had to shoot, faces he still sees in his dreams. Both Alvin and his companion shed tears of repentance.

Camping next to a Catholic cemetery, Alvin is offered a home-cooked meal by the priest who comes out to join him. The priest happened to be visiting the hospital when Lyle was brought in following his stroke. "He didn't mention having a brother, though," the priest comments. "Neither one of us has had a brother for some time," replies Alvin.

The pilgrim recalls how he and Lyle, growing up on a hardscrabble farm, turned their chores into games to make the winter go by more quickly. They talked for hours while watching the stars, and daydreamed about places they would go someday. "We talked each other through growing up," Alvin recalls.

By the time Alvin arrives at Lyle's ramshackle house, he has thoroughly repented of the pride that separated him from his brother. He has done the penance of a five-week pilgrimage in often cold and rainy weather on a stiff tractor seat. And he has borne the shame of being seen by many on his eccentric conveyance.

Death waits patiently in the wings throughout *The Straight Story*. When Alvin's first lawnmower breaks down, he hitches a ride on a bus going to the Grotto. There we glimpse a white crucifix among the outdoor Stations of the Cross. At the cemetery, Alvin rests near the French trappers who made their own arduous journeys through the Midwest. Images of harvest time remind us that we, like the Straight brothers, will one day face our own final autumn.

. . . . .

"Not knowing when the dawn will come, I open every door."
—Emily Dickinson

. . . . .

Contemporary Wisdom

As the two concelebrants processed down the aisle, I noticed that the visitor walked with a slight limp and was wearing large white sneakers. "Rather odd for a Jesuit," I remember thinking, "especially such a distinguished one." Walter J. Burghardt, S.J., preacher and author, was to be the guest homilist on the occasion of our pastor's twenty-fifth anniversary of ordination.

Despite his loftiness, I felt an immediate kinship with Walter Burghardt. At the time, I was walking with a cane and wearing one of those cumbersome surgical shoes that come only in size fifteen. In his homily on the priesthood of Jesus, of all the faithful, and of the ordained, the preacher admitted, "We are saddest when our homilies leave you cold." He spoke of standing at the altar and weeping that "only thirty percent of Catholics share in this experience with us Sunday after Sunday." And he revealed that, at eighty-four after fifty-eight years as a priest, he found "aging hard to enjoy alone."

Meeting with our guest in the rectory after Mass, I was greeted with an unexpected hug. (I had assumed that all Jesuits were too restrained for such signs of affection for strangers.) We promptly compared our mutual "disabilities": his pronated left foot in a metal brace, and my post-operative right foot with its newly straightened toes. He insisted, however, that these imperfect feet were "beautiful because they bring good news."

Had Walter Burghardt not come to our parish on that Pentecost Sunday in May 1999, I might never have read in 2000 his new book, *Long Have I Loved You: A Theologian Reflects on His Church*. In it, the author meditates on his life of service in the church, and on the death for which his age makes him a certain candidate. Although he is familiar with Elizabeth Kubler-Ross's five stages of dying (denial, anger, bargaining with God, depression and acceptance), Burghardt realizes that knowledge alone will be inadequate. He knows he will be "anguishing toward a death which is more than resignation, a death I hope will be my final 'I do,' my last gift to the Lord of life."[6]

. . . . .

"IN YOUR INNER LIFE YOU WILL NOT WASTE AWAY EVEN WHEN YOUR LIFE HAS BECOME WEIGHED DOWN WITH YEARS."
—Augustine of Hippo

. . . . .

"...FOR LOVE IS STRONG AS DEATH."
—Song of Solomon 8:6

. . . . .

Like most of us, the author fears the blank face of death. He dreads being broken and vanishing from the "reach and touch" of those who love him. He hopes for a "fresh conversion to the risen Christ" before death makes its claim on him. If he has to die in a hospital, he prays it is a Catholic one in which his caretakers will share his faith and there will be a crucifix on the wall above his head. Seeing that sacramental, he will be moved to pray "This is my body [and it is] given for you" (Luke 22:19).

Burghardt quotes from a letter written to him by John and Denise Carmody in July 1995. The Catholic coauthors were sharing with friends how John was coping with a malignant tumor of the bone marrow. Carmody had dedicated himself to full and grateful living "while practicing the art of dying." Reflecting on how Jesus knew from within our human experience of "learning to die while loving living," Carmody says:

> Trying therefore to become, not callous about pain or death, not presumptuous, but free of their power to loom up as frightening idols and block out the far greater reality of God.... So we wait, letting our aging, sickening bodies instruct us as much as our minds, and remembering that we have not been called servants but friends.[7]

With endearing candor, Walter Burghardt tells us how much he dreads death's destruction of the "I." He lists a paragraph full of his particular loves and passions (Handel's *Messiah*, spaghetti bolognese, Augustine's *City of God*). Then he says exactly what any one of us could truthfully say:

> This "I" God will not replace, cannot replace. I am not just some one; I am this one. Through [all my] years for good or ill, I have touched, been touched by, a

"NOW GOD COMES TO THEE...AS THE SHEAVES IN HARVEST,... ALL OCCASIONS INVITE HIS MERCIES, AND ALL TIMES ARE HIS SEASONS."
—John Donne

"IF ANYTHING IS SACRED, THE HUMAN BODY IS SACRED."
—Walt Whitman

whole little world. When I die, this warm
pulsating flame of human living and loving will die with me.[8]

Seeking counselors who will help him master the art of
dying, the theologian turns to the early Greek Fathers of the
Church. Methodius, for example, believed that death was a
remedy for sin. As long as we occupy our bodies, sin's hidden
roots will remain in us. Comparing God to a master craftsman, Methodius draws an analogy between a sculptor who
melts down a gold statue that has been marred. The craftsman then remolds the statue to a flawless condition. This,
Methodius says, is what happens to us in the resurrection.[9]

Among the others who inform Burghardt's understanding is Gregory of Nyssa. He, too, views death as the means
by which we are "resolved into earth, in order to part with
the sordidness" in which sin has involved us. Gregory
writes: "For this is the resurrection: dissolution and regener-
ation of our nature to its primordial state."[10]

Walter Burghardt knows that his dying began eighty-
eight years ago and that he has participated in Jesus' dying
by sharing his cross throughout that time. He does not seek
to be resigned to death as an inevitable and undesirable end.
His goal is to actively say "yes" to it, just as Jesus assented
to his death on the cross: "Then he bowed his head and
gave up his spirit" (John 19:30).

Like us, the Jesuit theologian expresses noble hopes
which are at times belied by earth's habitual pull. There is
much he loves in the privileged life he has lived, much he is
not ready to do without. Memories of his father's and brother's
deaths of cancer, and of his mother's degeneration from
Alzheimer's disease instill fear in his own heart. These are
paths he abhors and does not want to contemplate walking.

Finally, Burghardt shrinks from the abstraction of the life
to come. His lifelong desire to see and understand the things
of God cannot be fully satisfied. There is frustration is
embracing the darkness. He takes comfort in a prayer of

. . . . .

"THERE IS NO
DEATH. ONLY A
CHANGE OF
WORLDS."
—Chief Seattle

. . . . .

Teilhard de Chardin, a prayer of seeking assimilation into the body of Jesus. Teilhard closes with the following paragraph:

> You are the irresistible and vivifying force, O Lord, and because yours is the energy, because, of the two of us, you are infinitely stronger, it is on you that falls the part of consuming me into the union that should weld us together. Vouchsafe, therefore, something more precious still than the grace for which all the faithful pray. It is not enough that I should die while communicating. *Teach me to treat my death as an act of communion.*[11]

I take solace in Walter Burghardt's honest expression of his fears and doubts. If he, priest and scholar, sometimes "shivers and shakes" when contemplating death, I can admit to quaking before the prospect of old age and losing my grip on this sweet life. Looking back at this renowned Jesuit's Christmas letter to friends, I am assured that his humor is still intact while his body parts slowly resign from active service. His report of one eye's macular degeneration, three root canals, and four broken toes sounds like an elderly comic's version of "An Antiquated Partridge in a Venerable Pear Tree." Can we doubt that Burghardt will greet death with a perceptive smile and a little soft-shoe routine in white sneakers?

. . . . .

"AND SO...IN THIS LIFE WE ARE PILGRIMS; WE SIGH IN FAITH FOR OUR TRUE COUNTRY WHICH WE ARE UNSURE ABOUT."
—Augustine of Hippo

. . . . .

"BLESSED BE GOD FOR OUR SISTER, THE DEATH OF THE BODY."
—Francis of Assisi

. . . . .

HOLY LAUGHTER

Fenced in by fear and trepidation, death would seem to be no laughing matter. But take a closer look. Maybe there is more space for smiling than we imagined. Those saints whose last words included "happy" could be giving us a clue about what to expect at the end of the line.

As a card-carrying member of the Fellowship of Merry Christians, I have for years collected jokes, cartoons and funny stories that elicit healing laughter. My collection is a final-aid kit filled with soothing potions. Proverbs tells us repeatedly that a cheerful heart is "good medicine" and "a continual feast" (17:22; 15:13; 15:15). We are reminded that "The human spirit will endure sickness; / but a broken spirit—who can bear?" (18:14).

When the Fellowship began publicizing a portrait called *Risen Christ by the Sea* painted by Jack Jewell, the response was overwhelmingly positive. The portrait depicted a decidedly unsolemn Jesus whose smile could illuminate New York City in a blackout. Viewers who sunned themselves in that smile felt a surge of resurrection joy. Terminally ill patients grinned back at this jubilant Shepherd who would soon lead them home. They imagined him taunting death and Satan with a triumphant, "The joke's on you, fellas!"

In the pages of the Fellowship's *Joyful Noiseletter,* I have found dozens of death-defying stories to save and share with those who need them. Archbishop John L. May contributed a favorite: The funeral of a veteran gambler was attended by many of his professional cronies. As the minister gave the eulogy, he observed, "Spike is not dead; he only sleeps." A voice from the back of the chapel responded, "I got a hundred that says he's dead."[12]

Another example: Pharmacist Cliff Thomas tells the story about a hardworking druggist who was so sick one morning that he could not report to work. His wife called the doctor's office to make an appointment. The receptionist informed her that they were so busy they could not fit the druggist in for at least two weeks. The frustrated caller remarked, "He could be dead by then!" "No problem," said the receptionist, "just have someone give us a call and we'll cancel the appointment."[13]

And no matter how many times we hear the anonymous story about the dying woman who wanted to be buried with her Bible in one hand and a fork in the other, we can still smile at her explanation. We, too, have been

. . . . .

"JESUS IS HERE, AND HE WANTS TO RESURRECT SOMEBODY!"
—Rumi

. . . . .

"I FIND ONLY ONE FAULT WITH YOU, DEATH: THAT YOU ARE TOO STINGY WITH THOSE WHO LONG FOR YOU, AND TOO LAVISH WITH THOSE WHO FLEE FROM YOU."
—Catherine of Genoa

. . . . .

instructed at countless church suppers to keep our forks after the main course is cleared away. We have not forgotten that "The best is yet to come."

To add a little tartness to my collection, I put away *The New Yorker* cartoons like homemade pickles in the cellar. For example: In a sketch of three tombstones, the one in the middle is inscribed in capital letters, "WHY ME?" (Barbara Smaller). I am tickled by a drawing of a man arriving at the pearly gates only to be forewarned by Saint Peter, "Bad timing—he's in one of his Old Testament moods today" (Charles Barsotti).

Among the saints whose witness assures me that holy laughter is as necessary on the deathbed as clean sheets is Thérèse of Lisieux. During her long and painful bout with tuberculosis, the young Carmelite occasionally unsheathed the sword of ironic humor. When Thérèse once refused a cup of broth offered by a sister Carmelite, the nun stomped off in a snit, complaining that Thérèse could not possibly be the saint she was rumored to be because she was not even a good religious. To this insult, Thérèse replied, "What a benefaction to hear on one's deathbed that one has not even been a proper nun!"[14]

When unable to stop coughing, she compared herself to a locomotive chugging into the station. "I'm arriving also at a station: heaven, and I'm announcing it!" she told her sisters.[15] Another time she was required to drink snail-syrup for medicinal purposes. Thérèse quipped that it was not a problem for her as long as she could not see their horns. She compared herself to ducklings who dine on snails. "Yesterday, I was acting like the ostriches," she added, "I was eating eggs raw!"[16]

Although Thérèse was eager to see Jesus, she did not pray that her sufferings would end. She commented that she was like a person with a lottery ticket who at least has a better chance of winning than the ticket-less person. "So I have a ticket, my illness, and I can keep up my hopes!"[17]

. . . . .

"HE WHO HAS THE COURAGE TO LAUGH IS AS MUCH A MASTER OF THE WORLD AS [SHE] WHO IS READY TO DIE."
—Giacomo Leopardi

. . . . .

"THE SECRET SOURCE OF HUMOR ITSELF IS NOT JOY BUT SORROW."
—Mark Twain

. . . . .

Thérèse endured terrible doubts, depression, and even despair during her final months. Yet when her sisters worried about whether her features would be contorted in an agonizing death, she told them not to be sad if that did happen. "For immediately afterwards," she said, "I'll have nothing but smiles."[18] The saint of the Little Way died saying, "My God...I love you!" with her characteristic exclamation point. Her eyes were "brilliant with peace and joy."[19]

Although she died over a century ago (1897), Thérèse of Lisieux continues to nourish us with the wit, patience and perseverance she practiced during her final illness.

Morrie Schwartz, a Jewish college professor, who died in 1995, offers us a similar witness of heroic deathbed virtue. Mitch Albom's book *Tuesdays with Morrie* allows us to eavesdrop on the lessons Schwartz shared with this former student.

My own copy of *Tuesdays* is stored in my final-aid kit. Morrie joins Thérèse and Thomas More as my patron saints of the dying. When the time comes, he will remind me of the following truths. Like Morrie, I pray I can:

- Be a bridge between the living and the dead by sharing whatever wisdom I have gained about living with purpose, love, and joy;

- Limit myself to a small (or medium-sized) daily dose of self-pity before focusing once again on living as well as I can;

- Have the wit to turn at least some of my embarrassing physical impairments into fodder for others' relieved laughter;

- Be able to squeeze out a quarter-ounce of humor when I begin to suspect that I might be walking in Job's ash-covered sandals. For example, when asked how he felt about God's testing Job with terrible sickness and loss, Morrie smiled and said, "I think, God overdid it."[20]

. . . . .

"IF THERE IS NO ONE IN THE JUDGMENT SEAT WITH A SENSE OF HUMOR, I'LL ASK FOR A CHANGE OF VENUE."
—Jimmy Walker

. . . . .

"IF SOME DIED AND OTHERS DID NOT, DEATH WOULD BE A TERRIBLE AFFLICTION."
—LaBruyere

. . . . .

- Attempt to obey the aphorism: "Don't let go too soon, but don't hang on too long."[21]

- Know for certain that death does not end my relationships with all those I love. We will go on loving each other beyond time and telling.

May those who are preparing for death as they read these pages be helped to answer: How will you comfort yourself and those who must let you go? What final insights will you share in writing, video or audiotape? How will you allow the *Risen Christ by the Sea* to shine in you?

REFLECT
What humorous or lighthearted moments in your life will you share with a family member who will give your eulogy?

How will you practice strengthening your belief in your own resurrection, as well as your desire to see God face to face?

PRAY
O Divine Comforter,
shield the imperiled heart,
the soul shadowed by death.
Comfort, comfort
all who are dying.
Give us blessed assurance.
Raise us up to the light.
Amen.

. . . . .

"LAUGHTER IS
GOD'S HAND ON
THE SHOULDERS
OF A TROUBLED
WORLD."
—Minnie Pearl

. . . . .

Be Comforted

1. Office for the Dead, Antiphon 1, Office of Readings, *Christian Prayer: The Liturgy of the Hours* (New York: Catholic Book Publishing Co., 1976), p. 1474.

2. Louis L. Martz, *Thomas More: Search for the Inner Man* (New Haven: Yale University Press, 1990), p. 81.

3. *St. Thomas More: Selected Letters*, ed. Elizabeth Frances Rogers (New Haven: Yale University Press, 1961), p. 237.

4. *Ibid.*, p. 238.

5. Richard Marius, *Thomas More: A Biography* (New York: Alfred A. Knopf, 1985), p. 488.

6. Walter J. Burghardt, S.J., *Long Have I Loved You: A Theologian Reflects on His Church* (Maryknoll, NY: Orbis Books, 2000), p. 370.

7. *Ibid.*, pp. 377–378.

8. *Ibid.*, p. 390.

9. *Ibid.*, p. 391.

10. *Ibid.*, p. 392.

11. *Ibid.*, p. 400.

12. *Joyful Noiseletter*, Fellowship of Merry Christians. Aug.-Sept. 1992, p. 2.

13. *Ibid.*, May 2003, p. 4.

14. Monica Furlong, *Thérèse of Lisieux* (New York: Pantheon Books, 1987), p. 112.

15. *St. Thérèse of Lisieux: Her Last Conversations*, John Clarke, O.C.D., trans. (Washington, D.C.: ICS Publications, 1977), p. 42.

16. *Ibid.*, p. 59.

17. *Ibid.*, p. 51.

18. *Ibid.*, p. 86.

19. *Ibid.*, p. 206.

20. Mitch Albom, *Tuesdays with Morrie: An Old Man, a Young Man, and Life's Greatest Lesson* (New York: Doubleday, 1997), p. 151.

21. *Ibid.*, p. 162.

Conclusion

"GOD IS OUR REFUGE AND STRENGTH,
A VERY PRESENT HELP IN TROUBLE."
—Psalm 46:1

A few years ago I was slogging through a depression, searching my memory for a reason to get out of bed. I reached for a volume by Ralph Waldo Emerson. A friend had sent me a collection of his bracing aphorisms. I had paid little attention to this nineteenth-century transcendental philosopher and lay preacher since my undergraduate days. That may be why his distinctive voice struck me with all the clarity of the Angelus bell.

No stranger to tragedy, Emerson suffered the death of his cherished first wife Ellen only sixteen months after their wedding. Later his five-year-old son Waldo died of scarlet fever. Later still his Concord home was badly damaged by fire. I include these facts as a reminder that the optimistic faith expressed by Emerson had been honed on hard trouble.

I was fortunate that my friend gave me not the full collection of Emerson's essays, the complexity and verbiage of which would have depressed me further. What I received instead was *Self-Reliance: The Wisdom of Ralph Waldo Emerson as Inspiration for Daily Living*. The editor, Richard Whelan, had judiciously picked all the shiniest apples from the tree and divided them into their thematic varieties: Spiritual Laws, Friendship, Character and so forth. All the reader had to do was select an apple, chew it thoroughly, and allow it to energize his or her life.

Ruminating over Emerson's aphorisms, I repeatedly came across the very message needed on a particular day. If I could not bring myself to face a confrontation, my mentor observed, "Fear is a bad counselor."[1] If I could not move on with my life in a new direction, he advised, "We cannot stay amid the ruins."[2]

When I was pitying my sorry state, Emerson noted, "No man [or woman] ever stated his [her] griefs as lightly as he [she] might."[3] If tempted to spill my troubles one more time into a sympathetic ear, the sage shook his head and instructed, "We gain the strength of the temptation we resist."[4]

As I absorbed the genial Emerson's wisdom, I began to anticipate each day's exposure to his teaching. The experience of anticipation of any kind was a sign of improvement. By the time I came upon the following insight, I had the capacity to believe it once again: "We are escorted on every hand through life by spiritual agents, and a beneficent purpose lies in wait for us."[5]

And I was comforted.

May the Spirit use these pages to lead you who are suffering loss, anger, anxiety, loneliness, sickness or the approach of death into the consolation only the Divine Comforter can give.

. . . . .

"JOY CAN SPRING LIKE A FLOWER, EVEN FROM THE CLIFFS OF DESPAIR."
—Anne Morrow Lindbergh

. . . . .

"NO MATTER HOW DEEP OUR DARKNESS, HE IS DEEPER STILL."
—Corrie ten Boom

. . . . .

"AND FINALLY, NEVER LOSE HOPE."
—Benedict of Nursia

. . . . .

NOTES

1. *Self-Reliance: The Wisdom of Ralph Waldo Emerson for Daily Living*, ed. Richard Whelan (New York: Bell Tower, 1991), p. 126.

2. *Ibid.*, p. 98.

3. *Ibid.*, p. 47.

4. *Ibid.*, p. 96.

5. *Ibid.*, p. 182.

Chapter 1
(Loss and Divorce)

Books

Day, Dorothy. *The Long Loneliness*. New York: Harper & Brothers, 1962.

Ford, Debbie. *Spiritual Divorce*. San Francisco: Harper, 2001.

Monbourquette, John. *How to Forgive: A Step-By-Step Guide*. Cincinnati: St. Anthony Messenger Press, 2000.

O'Donnell, Karen. *Praying Through Your Divorce*. Cincinnati: St. Anthony Messenger Press, 2000.

Rolheiser, Ronald. *The Holy Longing: The Search for a Christian Spirituality*. New York: Doubleday, 1999.

Videos

Dream's End: Spiritual Recovery from Divorce and Separation. St. Louis, Mo.: Videos with Values, 1995.

Entertaining Angels: The Dorothy Day Story. The story of Dorothy Day's early adult years. Burbank, Calif: Warner Home Video, 1997.

Far from Heaven. A 1950s marriage falls apart when both partners face reality. Los Angeles: New Line Home Video, 2002.

Life as a House. A divorced architect with cancer reconciles with ex-wife and son. Burbank, Calif: Warner Home Video, 2002.

Mrs. Doubtfire. Comedy in which a divorced father remains in the lives of his children and reconciles with his ex-wife. Beverly Hills, Calif: Fox Video, 1996.

Parenthood. Comedy in which divorced and married members of an extended family cope with their mutual problems. Universal City, Calif: MCA Universal Home Video, 1990.

Scenes from a Marriage. Bergman film chronicling a marriage that ends in divorce but the relationship perseveres as a source of mutual comfort. New York: Columbia Pictures Home Entertainment, 1983.

Chapter 2
(Anger at Injustice)

Books

Bernardin, Joseph Cardinal. *The Gift of Peace: Personal Reflections.* Chicago: Loyola Press, 1997.

King, Martin Luther, Jr. *The Trumpet of Conscience.* San Francisco: Harper, 1967.

Kurtz, Ernest and Katherine Ketcham. *The Spirituality of Imperfection.* New York: Bantam Books, 1992.

Merton, Thomas. *The Wisdom of the Desert.* New York: New Directions, 1960.

Nhat Hanh, Thich. *Being Peace.* Berkeley: Parallax Press, 1987.

Romero, Oscar. *The Violence of Love.* Foreword by Henri Nouwen. Farmington, Pa: Plough Publishing House, 1998.

Videos

Bernardin. Story of Joseph Cardinal Bernardin and his reconciliation with his accuser. Journey/Frost, 1998.

Dead Man Walking. Sister Helen Prejean's ministry to death row prisoners. New York: PolyGram Video, 1996.

Erin Brockovich. A paralegal's battle against environmental injustice. Universal City: Universal, 2000.

Evelyn. Irish father channels anger into a legal battle to regain custody of his children. Santa Monica: MGM Home Entertainment, 2003.

Friendly Persuasion. Quaker family tries to live by the nonviolence they profess in the Civil War. Burbank: Warner Home Video, 1988.

Gandhi. The Mahatma practices nonviolence in leading India to freedom from British rule. Burbank: RCA/Columbia Pictures Home Video, 1982.

Philadelphia. Gay attorney with AIDS is fired and directs his anger into legal search for justice. Burbank: Columbia TriStar Home Video, 1994.

To Kill a Mockingbird. Atticus Finch demonstrates heroic anger-management in professional and personal life. Universal City: MCA Home Video, 1981.

Chapter 3
(Anxiety)

Books

Kushner, Harold S. *Living a Life That Matters: Resolving the Conflict Between Conscience and Success.* New York: Alfred A. Knopf, 2001.

Luebering, Carol. *A Retreat with Job and Julian of Norwich: Trusting That All Will Be Well.* Cincinnati: St. Anthony Messenger Press, 1995.

Nouwen, Henri J.M. *Here and Now: Living in the Spirit* (audiobook) Cincinnati: St. Anthony Messenger Press, 2001.

Oliver, Mary. *New and Selected Poems.* Boston: Beacon Press, 1992.

Remen, Rachel Naomi. *My Grandfather's Blessings: Stories of Strength, Refuge, and Belonging.* New York: Riverhead Books, 2000.

Videos

Adaptation. A writer is hobbled by anxieties about his own performance and the success of his brother. Culver City, Calif.: Columbia TriStar Home Entertainment, 2003.

Frontline: Faith & Doubt at Ground Zero. How the tragedy of 9/11 affected Americans' faith. Alexandria, Va.: PBS Home Video, 2002.

The Hours. Multileveled story of how three women and a gay man respond to their anxieties. Hollywood: Paramount, 2003.

Manhattan. Woody Allen comedy about a neurotic journalist dealing with mid-life crisis. New York: MGM/UA Home Video, 1984.

Monsignor Quixote. A priest explores his doubts and anxieties on a journey prompted by his elevation to monsignor. New York: HBO Studios, 1997.

Parenthood. Comedy in which Steve Martin's character displays common anxieties of parents and spouses, as well as grown sons and daughters. Universal City: MCA Universal Home Video, 1990.

The Pink Panther Strikes Again. Comedy in which anxiety-ridden Inspector Dreyfus is once again bested by the bumbling Inspector Clouseau. Culver City, Calif.: MGM/UA, 1990.

Be Comforted

Chapter 4
(Loneliness)

Books

De Mello, Anthony. *Awareness: The Perils and Opportunities of Reality.* Edited by J. Francis Stroud, S.J. New York: Doubleday, 1992.

Hopkins, Gerard Manley. *Poems of Gerard Manley Hopkins.* Edited by W.H. Gardner. New York: Oxford University Press, 1948.

Powell, John, S.J. *Happiness Is an Inside Job.* Allen, Tex.: Tabor Publishing, 1989.

Powers, Jessica. *Selected Poetry of Jessica Powers.* Edited by Regina Siegfried and Robert Morneau. Kansas City, Mo.: Sheed & Ward, 1989.

Teresa of Avila. *The Way of Perfection.* Translated and edited by E. Allison Peers. Garden City, N.Y.: Image Books, 1964.

Videos

Cast Away. How a man stranded on a deserted island for four years creatively copes with loneliness. Beverly Hills: 20th Century Fox Home Entertainment, 2002.

Central Station. Brazilian film in which a retired teacher is drawn out of loneliness and selfishness by a young orphan. Culver City, Calif.: Columbia TriStar Home Video, 1999.

Diary of a Country Priest. Georges Bernanos' story of a terminally-ill young priest who is a misfit in his rural parish. New York: Kino International/Kino Video, 2001.

The Elephant Man. Disfigured and diseased John Merrick overcomes the loneliness of being a sideshow freak. Hollywood: Paramount Home Video, 1981.

Jane Eyre. Charlotte Bronte's story of a plain governess who does not allow loneliness to overcome her conscience. Burbank: Buena Vista Home Video, 1996.

My Big Fat Greek Wedding. Comedy about a thirty-year-old single woman who breaks out of her family circle to find a decidedly non-Greek husband. New York: HBO Home Video, 2002.

Remains of the Day. A repressed butler and a head housekeeper on an English estate suffer the loneliness of unexpressed love. Burbank: Columbia TriStar Home Video, 1994.

Planes, Trains and Automobiles. Comedy in which a widowed salesman who disguises his loneliness is welcomed into a family's Christmas celebration. Hollywood: Paramount, 1987.

Chapter 5
(Sickness)

Books

Dickinson, Emily. *Collected Poems of Emily Dickinson.* New York: Gramercy Books, 1982.

Eckhart, Meister. *Meister Eckhart.* Translated by Raymond Bernard Blakney. New York: Harper & Row, 1941.

Hutchinson, Gloria. *A Retreat with Hopkins and Hildegard: Turning Pain into Power.* Cincinnati: St. Anthony Messenger Press, 1995.

Frost, Robert. *The Poetry of Robert Frost.* Edited by Edward Connery Lathem. New York: Holt, Rinehart and Winston, 1969.

Kreeft, Peter. *Making Sense Out of Suffering.* Ann Arbor, Mich.: Servant Books, 1986.

Oliver, Mary. *New and Selected Poems.* Boston: Beacon Press, 1992.

Willig, Jim. *Lessons from the School of Suffering: A Young Priest with Cancer Teaches Us How to Live.* With Tammy Bundy. Cincinnati: St. Anthony Messenger Press, 2001.

Videos

My Left Foot: The Story of Christy Brown. Christy Brown copes with cerebral palsy. New York: HBO Video, 1990.

One True Thing. How an ordinary woman's final illness affects her husband and daughter. Universal City: Universal, 1998.

On Golden Pond. An eighty-year-old retired professor and his wife deal with his early dementia. Van Nuys: LIVE Home Video, 1993.

Sr. Thea: Her Own Story. Film on Sister Thea Bowman's life and death. St. Louis, Mo.: Videos with Values.

Terms of Endearment. A woman's final illness is an opportunity for truth telling and reconciliation in her family. Boston: DVS Home Video, 1993.

When Bad Things Happen to Good People. Film based on Rabbi Harold S. Kushner's best-selling book. St. Louis, Mo.: Videos with Values, 1992.

Wit. A professor undergoes experimental cancer treatment with the help of John Donne's "Holy Sonnets" and her own strength of will. A difficult film that offers more challenge than comfort. New York: HBO Home Video, 2001.

Chapter 6
(Death)

Books
Albom, Mitch. *Tuesdays with Morrie.* New York: Doubleday, 1997.

Burghardt, Walter. *Long Have I Loved You: A Theologian Reflects on His Church.* Maryknoll, N.Y.: Orbis Books, 2000.

Groves, Richard. *The Sacred Art of Dying: Living with Hope* (audiobook). Cincinnati: St. Anthony Messenger Press, 2000.

Martz, Louis L. *Thomas More: The Search for the Inner Man.* New Haven: Yale University Press, 1990.

More, St. Thomas. *St. Thomas More: Selected Letters.* Edited by Elizabeth Frances Rogers. New Haven: Yale University Press, 1961.

Nouwen, Henri J.M. *Our Greatest Gift: A Meditation on Dying and Caring* (read by Murray Bodo, O.F.M.). Cincinnati: St. Anthony Messenger Press, 2001.

Therese of Lisieux. *St. Therese of Lisieux: Her Last Conversations.* Translated by John Clarke, O.C.D. Washington, D.C.: ICS Publications, 1977.

Videos
A Man for All Seasons. Film version of the play by Robert Bolt on More's faithful life and death. Burbank: RCA/Columbia Picture Home Video, 1987.

It's a Wonderful Life. Classic film in which a man discovers the great difference his life has made to his family and community. Los Angeles: Media Home Entertainment, 1981.

Jesus of Montreal. A young actor in a Passion play takes the Gospels literally and dies in character as Jesus. New York: Orion Home Video, 1991.

Life Is Beautiful. An Italian Jewish father gives his life in the process of shielding his five-year old son from the reality of a Nazi concentration camp. Burbank: Miramax Home Entertainment, 2000.

The Seventh Seal. Bergman film reflecting on life and death as symbolized by a chess match between the Knight and Death. New York: Janus Films, Home Vision Cinema, 1998.

The Straight Story. True story of Alvin Straight's pilgrimage to be reconciled with his ailing brother. Burbank: Walt Disney Home Video, 1999.

Shadowlands. True story of how author C.S. Lewis and his wife Joy cope with her death. New York: HBO Home Video, 1994.

Tuesdays with Morrie. Made-for-TV film of the book by Mitch Albom in which Morrie Schwartz shares his wisdom about living and dying. Burbank: Touchstone Home Video, 1999.